THE TWELVE SPIRITUAL LAWS OF MONEY

GOD'S BLUEPRINT FOR FINANCIAL FREEDOM

THE TWELVE SPIRITUAL LAWS OF MONEY

GOD'S BLUEPRINT FOR FINANCIAL FREEDOM

ANANIAH CLARK

BlackaWare Publishing, LLC, Charlotte, North Carolina

BlackaWare Publishing
4833 Berewick Town Center Drive
Suite E, PMB 134
Charlotte, NC 28273
www.blarkawarepublishing.com

© 2026 Ananiah Clark
Cover design by Ananiah Clark

Published by BlackaWare Publishing 02 /01/2026

Library of Congress Control Number:2026902429
ISBN: Paperback: 979-8-9989891-7-9
ISBN: ePub: 979-8-9989891-6-2

All rights reserved. No part of this publication may be reproduced, distributed, or transmitted in any form or by any means, including photocopying, recording, or other electronic or mechanical methods, without the prior written permission of the publisher or author, except in the use of brief quotations embodied in critical reviews and certain other noncommercial uses permitted by copyright laws.

Although every precaution has been taken to verify the accuracy of the information contained herein, the author and publisher assume no responsibility for any errors or omissions. No liability is assumed for damages that may result from the use of information contained within.

Printed in the United States of America on acid-free paper.

Because of the dynamic nature of the Internet, any web addresses or links contained in this book may have changed since publication and may no longer be valid.

Contents

Introduction 1
Chapter One: The Spiritual Law of Acquisition 9
Chapter Two: The Habits of Focus and Effort 15
Chapter Three: The Spiritual Law of Tithing 23
Chapter Four: The Habits of Consistency and Faith 29
Chapter Five: The Spiritual Law of Accumulation 37
Chapter Six: Protection against Financial Storms 43
Chapter Seven: The Spiritual Law of Budgeting 51
Chapter Eight: The Habits of Discipline and Self-Control 57
Chapter Nine: The Spiritual Law of Intentionality 65
Chapter Ten: The Habits of Determination and Persistence 73
Chapter Eleven: The Spiritual Law of Sowing and Reaping 81
Chapter Twelve: The Habits of Patience and Diligence 87
Chapter Thirteen: The Spiritual Law of Manifestation 95
Chapter Fourteen: Spiritual Law of Purpose 103
Chapter Fifteen: The Spiritual Law of Faithfulness............ 109
Chapter Sixteen: The Spiritual Law of Reciprocity 117
Chapter Seventeen: The Spiritual Law of Detachment 125
Chapter Eighteen: The Spiritual Law of Transference....... 131
Chapter Nineteen: Teach What You Have Been Taught... 135
About The Author 139

Introduction

On a cool evening, I walked into the Financial Stewardship Workshop and felt the weight of a people who had been carrying financial burdens for far too long. The room was already full, with every folding chair occupied by stories that stretched across generations.

There were single mothers whose exhaustion sat heavy beneath their eyes, young men and women trying to rewrite their future after outrunning the streets, married couples pinned beneath the quiet pressure of overdue bills, elders raising grandchildren on fixed incomes, and young college students just starting their financial journey.

Some had once earned well but lost it through poor decisions. Others had never had enough to know how to manage it. Believers, skeptics, tithers, and nonchurch-goers, all sat shoulder to shoulder, united by one unspoken truth:

"Why does it seem like money keeps slipping through my hands faster than I can hold it?"

I stood there, not as a preacher trying to impress anybody, but as a Black man who had seen enough, lived enough, lost enough, and learned enough to tell the truth plainly.

I raised my Bible and, knowing full well the history pressing against our people, said:

"God did not create you for poverty.

"He did not call you to lack.

"His will is that you walk in abundance. Spiritually, financially, and generationally."

For as long as I can remember, African Americans have carried financial struggle like it was our birthright. We stretched nickels into dollars. We survived on leftovers and miracles. We tithed faithfully but still lived broke. Our grandparents shouted their way through service while the bills still waited at home. Somewhere along the line, struggle was normalized, and faith was separated from financial wisdom.

But Scripture tells a different story. From Abraham to Joseph, from Proverbs to the teachings of Yahshua, the Bible reveals a blueprint for money: how to earn it with purpose, manage it with wisdom, multiply it with discipline, and leave a legacy that blesses generations.

The problem is not that God's people lack instruction, it's that His financial principles have been buried beneath systemic oppression, generational trauma, and harmful money habits that are keeping African-American communities in cycles of lack.

This cycle is not God's will.

And it must be broken.

But before anything can change, we must confront the truth head-on. For too long, money has been mishandled, misunderstood, and mismanaged in Black households. It's the one subject the church avoids, the family argues about, and the heart fears in silence. We were taught to stretch what little we had, but not to build anything lasting. We learned how to survive, but never how to strategize. We relied on emotion when we needed financial education. We held on to hope, but we never developed the habits that turn hope into stability.

Yet the Word of God gives us over 2,000 Scriptures on how we should manage the money God places in our hands. These principles don't just fix budgets; they break chains. They heal shame. They restore hope. They rebuild families and they create Black wealth where none existed before.

That is the purpose of this book.

The Twelve Spiritual Laws of Money: God's Blueprint for Financial Freedom is not a prosperity scheme. It is not a get-rich-quick trick. It is not spiritual manipulation.

It is a return.

A restoration.

A reclamation of the financial wisdom God intended for His people from the beginning.

In this book, we journey through twelve spiritual laws:

1. The Law of Acquisition
2. The Law of Tithing
3. The Law of Accumulation
4. The Law of Budgeting
5. The Law of Intentionality
6. The Law of Sowing and Reaping
7. The Law of Manifestation
8. The Law of Purpose
9. The Law of Faithfulness
10. The Law of Reciprocity

11. The Law of Detachment

12. The Law of Transference

Each law is rooted in Scripture, shaped by real experience, and crafted to help you unlearn the lies you inherited and replace them with divine wisdom that builds abundance.

While these laws of money can transform anyone's life, this message carries a special urgency for Black America. We may not have chosen the economic barriers forced upon us, but we can choose how we rise beyond them. We can choose to break the cycles that tried to claim us. We can choose to teach our children the truths we were never taught. We can choose to build legacies instead of liabilities. Our history may explain our struggle, but it does not determine our future.

Some of us are the first generation with the chance to do this.

And because of that, we must not fail.

This is not merely a book. It is a call to:

Shift our strategy.

Stop surviving and start building.

Break generational poverty and establish generational prosperity.

Align your finances with God's purpose so that your life, your family, and your community are transformed.

The goal is not simply to become rich. The goal is to become whole.

Because the time has come for African Americans to step boldly into God's blueprint for financial freedom.

No more delay.

No more excuses.

No more living beneath what God intended.

This is the moment to rise, rebuild, and reclaim our covenant promise.

Now, let's build the kind of wealth that honors God and establishes a legacy so strong that generations to come will speak your name with gratitude.

THE FIRST
SPIRITUAL LAW OF MONEY

CHAPTER ONE

The Spiritual Law of Acquisition

I remember the room during the first meeting of the Financial Stewardship Workshop: the way silence sat on everyone like a heavy coat, the way eyes followed me with a mixture of hunger and hesitation. People had shown up because something in them knew they were created for more, but life had taught them to expect less. And as I stood there with my Bible open, I felt the weight of what God wanted to say through me. Not just to the people sitting in those chairs, but to anyone who has ever felt financially defeated, spiritually disconnected, or culturally conditioned to believe that abundance was meant for someone else.

I took a breath and looked at each face. I saw people who worked long hours. People who prayed long prayers. People who loved God deeply yet struggled silently when it came to money. I could feel their expectation, and I knew this moment required truth spoken with authority but carried with compassion.

So, I began with the foundation, not a principle I invented, not a motivational idea, but a spiritual law that existed long before any of us took our first breath.

Looking out at the group, I named the foundation. "It's called 'The Spiritual Law of Acquisition.'"

Then I paused for a moment, letting the words settle in their mind.

Next, I read aloud **Deuteronomy 8:18**, which states: *But thou shalt remember the Lord thy God: for it is He that giveth thee power to get wealth, that He may establish His covenant which He sware unto thy fathers, as it is this day.*

I recited it as a Scripture to memorize, and asked them to write down the verse in their notebooks. I had delivered the message like a law etched into the structure of creation itself. Because that is exactly what it is: a divine decree governing how wealth enters the life of a believer. And if we ever hope to walk in God's financial freedom, we must begin by acknowledging the One who authored wealth in the first place.

I walked slowly across the room, tapping the Bible in my hand—not for theatrics but because I needed the people in the room to hear this truth deep in their spirit: money does not start with you. Wealth does not start with your paycheck. Opportunity does not start with your talent, your job title, your degree, or your hustle. Money begins with God. He is the Creator, the Source, and the Owner of it all.

The silver is mine and the gold is mine, He declares in **Haggai 2:8**. *The earth is the Lord's and everything in it*, proclaims **Psalm 24:1**.

Everything you see, touch, earn, or hope for, belongs to Him first. And somehow, somewhere along the way, we were taught to believe that everything starts with our struggle. But that is a lie that must be broken.

I could feel the attitude in the room shift as this truth settled in. Because deep down, many of us have spent our entire lives chasing money as though we were orphans in this world who have been forgotten and overlooked without access to anything unless we fought for every inch. And I understand that feeling.

As Black people in America, we have inherited narratives of scarcity, survival, and generational lack.

We watched our parents stretch dollars.

We watched our grandparents live through systems designed to strip them of ownership, opportunity, and access.

And without realizing it, we internalized those experiences as identity.

We began to think that wealth was always for someone else. That blessing always skipped over us.

That "just enough" was the best life we could ever hope for.

But I did not come to cosign that story. I came to break it.

I stated my thoughts with the full conviction of a man who has wrestled with God and has come out with revelation:

"You belong to a covenant people. The God who empowered Abraham to prosper, who opened wells for Isaac during famine, who increased Jacob wealth, who positioned Joseph in places he wasn't even supposed to be, that same God is your Father. That same covenant rests on you. You do not come from a people destined to live in lack; you come from a lineage designed to demonstrate God's blessing on the earth."

I looked at the group and asked, "What if the very ideas you keep dismissing are instructions from God?

"What if the business you keep dreaming about, the book you've been afraid to write, the investment you've been contemplating, the workshop you've imagined hosting, what if none of that is random?

"What if that is God whispering to you, trying to move you into the flow of divine provision?"

Immediately the room grew still. Because people know the truth when they hear it, even if they've spent years running from it.

The reality is simple: many of us pray for miracles while ignoring instructions.

We ask God to open doors while refusing to walk through the ones He already placed before us.

We wait for signs while dismissing the opportunities He keeps sending our way.

And I felt compelled to say it plainly:

"Obedience activates blessing.

"Not talent.

"Not luck.

"Not connections.

"Obedience."

Abraham obeyed and was blessed with the power to get wealth.

Isaac obeyed and was blessed with the power to get wealth.

Jacob obeyed and was blessed with the power to get wealth.

Moses, David, Solomon—every one of them walked in supernatural abundance not because they were perfect, but because they obeyed God's voice when it didn't make sense.

So, I shared with them what I want to share with you in this book:

"It's your turn.

"Your turn to obey God's instructions.

"Your turn to build what no one in your family has ever built.

"Your turn to walk in the kind of financial freedom your ancestors prayed for but never lived long enough to see.

"You may not have inherited money, but you can create the inheritance.

"You may not come from wealth, but wealth can come from you.

"And the moment you recognize that the power to acquire wealth is not in your hands but in God's, you will never again confuse the blessing with the Source."

As the workshop session closed, I announced that next time we would talk about focus and effort because once you recognize God as the Source, you must learn how to discipline your mind and direct your energy toward the purpose of God.

But tonight, I needed them to walk away with this truth engraved in their spirit:

"You were never created to chase money.

"You were created to partner with God, to walk in His covenant, and to manifest His provision on the earth.

"The power to acquire wealth is already in you, not because of who you are, but because of who your Father is. When you truly grasp that truth, everything in your life begins to shift. Your mind opens. Your plans become clearer. Ideas and inspiration flow with purpose. And you step into the God-given ability to create, build, and produce wealth."

CHAPTER TWO

The Habits of Focus and Effort

When the financial stewardship workshop gathered again, a different kind of alertness was among the attendees in the room. They were sitting forward in their chairs, not slouched, not drifting, but ready, ready in a way only truth can make you ready. I could see it in their eyes. The first spiritual law of money had unsettled something, awakened something, clarified something. So, I looked at them and said what the Holy Spirit had already placed on my heart:

"Now that you understand God gives you the power to get wealth, you must learn how to recognize when He's trying to give it to you."

Because it is one thing to know God is the Source; it is another thing to notice when the Source is speaking. So, I told them plainly that God whispers, but the world screams.

The noise of this generation, like notifications, endless scrolling, gossip, stress, and distractions wrapped in entertainment, has made it almost impossible for many of us to hear God clearly. And the tragedy is not that God isn't speaking. The tragedy is that His people have grown so accustomed to noise that silence feels unnatural.

But divine instruction rarely arrives in chaos; it comes in the stillness of a focused mind.

Some of us are begging God for a blessing we are too distracted to receive.

We want clarity while living in confusion.

We want direction while living in distraction.

We want a word from God but don't slow down long enough to hear the sentence.

I spoke with the credence of someone who has had to fight for his own stillness:

Focus is not a suggestion, it's a spiritual discipline.

Focus sharpens your discernment.

Focus makes you aware of divine patterns.

Focus connects God's Word to your situation.

Focus is what lets you notice the difference between a random thought and an inspired idea.

I looked at the women in the room: warriors who carried families, held communities together, poured into everyone but themselves, and I told them that some of their greatest assignments have already been revealed but drowned out by the noise of digital life.

So many of our sisters have Kingdom businesses growing inside them like home healthcare agencies, beauty services, childcare centers, nonprofits for girls and women, but every time God tries to whisper instructions, the phone buzzes, a video plays, a notification pops up, and the seed never has a chance to root—not because they didn't receive instruction, but because they couldn't hear it long enough to trust it.

Then I turned to the men: the ones society tells to be providers while never teaching them how to be visionaries.

Many of them received business ideas years ago, but the weight of life buried them—not because they lacked anointing, but because they lost focus. And buried ideas are not dead ideas. They're simply waiting for the initiation of your attention.

The Holy Spirit is your financial coach, but even the best coach can't help a player who won't look up from the sidelines. Focus is how you stay in the game.

But focus alone is not enough. Because God can give you vision, but He will not complete the assignment for you.

So, I noted, "Once God shows you the plan, you must move."

That's where the habit of effort comes in, not the effort society glorifies—the kind that burns out people and leaves them empty—but divine effort: the consistent, disciplined, obedient kind of movement that lets Heaven know you are serious.

Effort is the part of faith that requires sweat.

Effort is the part of obedience that exposes your fears.

Effort is what transforms possibility into reality.

And I pointed out the truth many churches avoid:

God will not drop a business into your lap.

He will not organize your ideas.

He will not build your credit score.

He will not write your book.

He will not attend your class.

He will not call your mentor.

He gives the seed, but you must cultivate the harvest.

God releases ideas, but He watches to see if you'll work them.

So, I asked questions they could not ignore:

"You prayed for financial breakthrough, but did you do your part?

"Did you write the plan?

"Did you save the first $50?

"Did you register the business name?

"Did you apply for the certification?

"Did you step into the room God has been nudging you toward?

"Too many of us call delays 'spiritual warfare' when the real battle is our lack of effort. Faith without works is dead because vision without action is disobedience dressed in hope."

I knew some of them were wrestling in their minds because there is always a voice that rises against you when you try to move in purpose. The voice that tells you you're not smart enough, not qualified enough, not young enough, not old enough, not connected enough. And I told them with all the authority in me that none of those voices are God's.

That is fear pretending to be logic.

That is doubt wearing the mask of caution.

That is the enemy trying to keep you from the wealth God already authorized.

I reminded them of what I wrote on the white board earlier:

Focus hears God.

Effort obeys God.

When those two habits meet, wealth begins to move in your direction.

You don't need a hundred ideas. You just need the one God has already given you, and the discipline to work it consistently.

And as the workshop session came to an end, I didn't want them leaving with excitement alone because excitement fades. Emotion evaporates. But understanding sticks.

So, I told them the truth that shaped my own life: God honors movement. He honors obedience. He honors the one who shows up day after day, even when the results aren't visible yet. Because effort is what pulls blessing out of the invisible into the visible. And when your faith is focused and your effort is consistent, Heaven responds with supernatural timing.

Before we dismissed for the evening, I let them know that during our next gathering we would go deeper into the second spiritual law of money—tithing—not as a church tradition but as a Kingdom strategy for transforming your financial life. And as they packed their belongings and walked toward the exit, I could see something different in their body language.

Focus had awakened them.

Effort was stirring them.

And faith...faith was beginning to move.

THE SECOND
SPIRITUAL LAW OF MONEY

CHAPTER THREE

The Spiritual Law of Tithing

When we gathered again for the following workshop session, people were serious. They weren't whispering. They weren't distracted. They weren't casually flipping through their notes. They were still, leaning in, waiting—not for information, but for truth. And the moment I opened my Bible, it was as if this ambience itself leaned in with them. Because the next spiritual law we were about to discuss is one that has blessed countless believers…and blocked countless more.

I looked at them and stated plainly, "Now that you understand that God gives you the power to get wealth, we must deal with the law that determines what God can trust you with." And then I slowly read **Proverbs 3:9:** *Honor the Lord with thy substance, and with the first fruits of all thine increase*.

People in the room didn't make a sound or a move. They knew where I was going, but they didn't know the depth of it yet.

So, I continued:

"This is the Spiritual Law of Tithing.

"Not a church rule.

"Not a pastor's preference.

"Not a denominational tradition.

"A spiritual law. A divine instruction. A covenant principle established by God Himself."

And I knew before I even explained it that many hearts in the room had already been shaped by misinformation. Because tithing is one of the most attacked teachings in the entire Kingdom of God. Our enemies don't attack what is irrelevant; they attack what is powerful. And tithing, when practiced with understanding, is one of the most powerful acts of worship a believer can engage in.

So, I spoke the truth: "The reason tithing is so misunderstood is because it has been poorly taught, abused in some settings, ignored in others, and surrounded by lies for generations. And when you misunderstand a spiritual law, you don't just lose clarity—you lose access."

I could see the faces of people who had wrestled with this very issue.

People who loved God, but lived in fear.

People who prayed for provision, but never understood why breakthrough never seemed to arrive.

People who had allowed social media, TikTok theologians, and wounded former church members to shape their beliefs more than Scripture itself.

And I told them what God had taught me long ago: ignorance doesn't make you foolish, but it does leave you vulnerable. You can be sincere, faithful, prayerful, and devoted—and still live beneath your divine provision if you resist the laws God established for your blessing.

I read **Malachi 3:10**—not with guilt, not with manipulation, but with the authority of God's Word. *"Bring the whole tithe* *into the storehouse," the Lord says, "and see if I will not open the windows of Heaven and pour out a blessing you won't have room enough to receive."*

This is the only place in Scripture where God tells His people, "Test me."

Imagine that. The God of creation, the God who spoke galaxies into existence, the God who never needs to prove Himself to anyone—inviting you to test Him, to try Him, to put His promise to work.

And I looked at a brother sitting in the second row and asked, "Do you know what that means? God is daring you to trust Him."

I reminded the group of Abraham, Isaac, and Jacob—not as distant historical figures, but as spiritual ancestors whose lives still speak.

These men were tithers.

These men were covenant keepers.

These men honored God with their first tenth and God honored them with abundance.

Abraham walked in wealth. Isaac walked in wealth. Jacob walked in wealth. Not because they were lucky or privileged or perfect, but because they obeyed the God who had chosen them. And that same God has chosen you.

There is no reason the blessings that flowed through their lives cannot flow through yours—unless you refuse to walk in the same obedience.

I then wrote an expression on the white board, and I let it sit there for group reflection:

Tithing = Covenant Trust

Because that is what tithing really comes down to. God does not need your money. He already owns everything. What He wants is your trust—your willingness to acknowledge Him first, not last.

To bring Him the first tenth, not the leftovers.

To show Him that you honor the Source more than the paycheck.

I reminded the people in the room that some of the very breakthroughs they've been praying for are jammed in the doorway of their own disobedience. Not because God is punishing them, but because they are out of alignment with His principles.

Then a young woman raised her hand, and her question echoed what many others were thinking: "Where should I bring my tithe?"

I opened the Bible and reread part of the Malachi verse: *Bring the whole tithe into the storehouse.*

God has already told us where. In Israel of the Old Testament, the storehouse was the place where the people brought the first tenth—the place where those who served God were supported, where the community was cared for, where the spiritual and physical needs of the people were met.

Today, the storehouse is the place that feeds you spiritually, covers you in prayer, teaches you the Word with integrity, and is actively doing God's work in the community.

And I had to tell the truth as I've lived it and seen it: fifty or sixty years ago, the storehouse was always the Black church. But today, much of the work that once flowed through the church has been carried by nonprofits—organizations rooted in Kingdom principles but operating beyond the four walls.

Many churches preach, but they no longer feed the homeless.

Many churches worship, but they no longer serve the needs of the poor.

Many churches gather, but they are no longer active in the community.

And because of this disconnect, many believers don't know where their tithes should go.

So, I said: "If your spiritual nourishment comes from the church, tithe there. If the work of justice, service, and compassion is being done through Kingdom-based nonprofits, you can split your tithe between the two—because both are doing the work of God in different ways.

"What matters is alignment—alignment with God's Word, God's will, and God's work.

"When you tithe into your storehouse, you are partnering with Heaven to meet earthly needs. You are placing your resources in God's hands and saying, 'Use this to build Your Kingdom.' You are ensuring that the place that feeds you spiritually is strong enough to feed others. And that act alone places you under the flow of divine protection and provision."

Before we dismissed, I noted something every believer must understand: don't wait until things get better before you start tithing. That's like waiting until you're healed to start taking the medicine. Tithing is the cure, not the celebration.

It builds discipline.

It builds faith.

It builds alignment.

And alignment is what opens the windows of Heaven.

I could see it in their faces: conviction mixing with hope, revelation mixing with possibility. And I knew then that some of them were about to walk into financial transformation they'd never imagined.

I closed the workshop session by saying that next time we would talk about consistency and faith because once you honor God with your first tenth, you must learn how to walk with Him daily, steadily, and faithfully.

The kind of faith that doesn't waver when circumstances shift.

The kind of consistency that turns spiritual knowledge into practical breakthrough.

And as they began packing their belongings, I could observe something rising in them—a quiet courage, a newfound understanding, a willingness to trust God on another level.

And that is the beginning of abundance.

CHAPTER FOUR

The Habits of Consistency and Faith

When we gathered again the following week, something in the workshop's atmosphere had shifted. You could feel the change before anyone spoke. The last workshop session on tithing had unsettled old beliefs and awakened new convictions, and the air carried the weight of people who were wrestling—not with me, but with God. Some had tithed for the first time. Some had repented for years of inconsistency. Others had gone home replaying every Scripture, every truth, every warning, and every promise. I saw it in their eyes as they took their seats. They weren't just attending a workshop anymore—they were beginning a transformation.

So, I stepped forward, Bible under my arm, and spoke with the clarity God had given me:

"Family, last week we dealt with tithing, but today we're going deeper. Because it is one thing to obey once, but something entirely different to build a lifestyle of obedience. Anyone can act on a moment of conviction. But it takes consistency and faith—habits, not feelings—to move into the realm of sustained blessing."

I could see people straighten up, sensing that this wasn't a lecture; it was a mirror for reflection. I opened the Word to **Galatians 6:9**, reading it slowly so no one missed its weight: *And let us not be weary in well doing: for in due season, we shall reap, if we faint not.*

Consistency is the unglamorous discipline of doing the right thing long enough for the right thing to bear fruit. The Kingdom doesn't function like a lottery. You don't tithe once and expect Heaven to explode. You tithe like a farmer plants seed—steadily, faithfully, intentionally. And the problem for many believers is not that they don't sow; it's that they don't sow long enough. They let impatience talk them out of faith. They start strong and quit early. And in the realm of the Spirit, quitting is often the difference between almost blessed and overwhelmingly blessed.

The enemy doesn't fight your giving; he fights your consistency. He knows he can't stop God from blessing you, so he tries to stop you from being blessable. He whispers discouragement, plants doubt, magnifies your bills, triggers your fears, and makes your circumstances look louder than God's promise. He understands that if he can get you to break your rhythm, you will break your harvest. Because consistency is not just discipline—it is spiritual warfare. It is your way of telling the enemy, "I believe God more than I believe my situation."

But consistency alone is not enough; you need faith to sustain it. So, I turned to **Hebrews 11:6** and reminded them that *it is impossible to please God without faith*.

Not difficult—not challenging—not unlikely. *Impossible*.

Faith is not an idea; it is a posture.

Faith tithes when the paycheck is tight because it trusts the God who provided the paycheck in the first place.

Faith gives the first 10 percent without hesitation because it believes that the God who opened the door once can open it again.

Faith wakes up on difficult mornings, looks at shrinking accounts or rising bills, and still says, "Lord, I trust You."

That is the kind of faith God rewards. Not emotional faith. Not convenient faith. Not seasonal faith. *Consistent faith.*

I recounted the situation of Sister Williams, a woman from my earlier ministry days who tithed faithfully when she had almost nothing. She didn't tithe out of abundance; she tithed out of dependence.

Month after month, she gave.

Month after month, she prayed.

Month after month, she trusted.

And slowly, her situation began to shift.

Unexpected income arrived. Problems resolved themselves. Favor found her. And eventually, she received a promotion she wasn't even qualified for. Her breakthrough didn't come from a single act—it came from a sustained habit, from a lifestyle of trust.

I reached under the podium and brought out a jar filled with smooth stones, saying:

"Every stone in this jar represents a month I tithed faithfully for more than twenty years. When I first began, the jar was empty—not impressive, not inspiring, not majestic—just empty. But month after month, stone by stone, obedience turned into pattern, and pattern turned into lifestyle, and lifestyle turned into spiritual strength.

"This is how I developed my 'Faith muscles.'

"And when storms came—and trust me, they came—I wasn't shaken because consistency had already built what crisis couldn't break."

Then I looked at them the way a father looks at his children when he knows they are about to step into something greater and said, "Family, if you ever want to experience supernatural stability in your money, you must create natural habits rooted in spiritual truth."

Consistency is the pattern that shapes your destiny. Faith is the power that sustains the pattern. Together, they form an unbreakable rhythm that Heaven responds to.

Because the truth is simple: tithing will never work for the inconsistent. And faith will never work for the fearful. But when consistency meets faith, the supernatural becomes natural, and the miraculous becomes normal. Not because God suddenly becomes powerful—but because you finally become aligned.

The room was silent, the kind of silence that lets you know hearts are being rebuilt and minds are being restructured. And I smiled because I could see what they couldn't see yet: the beginnings of a people learning to walk in the financial rhythm of Heaven.

So, before they packed up their belongings, I told them that next time we gather, we're stepping into the third spiritual law of money—accumulation—because once you honor God and once you build habits of consistency and faith, you must learn how to multiply what He entrusts to your hands.

And as people walked out, quiet but strengthened, I knew something had taken root.

Something steady.

Something powerful.

Something God could build on.

THE THIRD
SPIRITUAL LAW OF MONEY

CHAPTER FIVE

The Spiritual Law of Accumulation

Morning sunlight poured through the tall windows of the Empowerment Center's room, painting it in a warm glow that felt almost symbolic. People filtered in with notebooks, coffee cups, and quiet anticipation. The last workshop session had stirred them—tithing had challenged their faith, exposed their habits, and awakened parts of them they had ignored for years. And now they were back, hungry again. Ready again. So, when I took my place at the front of the room, Bible tucked under my arm, and the white board behind me already marked with the words:

Tithing → Saving → Investing

I knew exactly what needed to be said.

I looked around the room, letting my eyes meet theirs one by one, and began, "Family, we've honored God with the first tenth. Now it's time to honor yourself. Because the next spiritual law, the one that has the power to shift your entire financial destiny, is the Spiritual Law of Accumulation. It is the law of paying yourself first."

I could see skepticism in some faces, curiosity in others, but all of them were listening. Continuing, I said plainly: "If you wait until after you've paid everyone else to set something aside for your future, you will never have anything left.

That's why so many of our people—generation after generation—live paycheck to paycheck. Not because they don't make money, but because they were never taught to keep any of it."

Marcus raised his hand, worry visible in his expression. "Pastor," he asked, "What if my 10 percent is only $20? That ain't gonna change my life."

I smiled because I've heard that question for decades, and the answer never changes. "Son," I told him, "Saving $20 every paycheck may not look like much today, but time is your partner. Discipline is your ally. The $20 is a seed, and seeds were never meant to stay seeds—they were meant to grow.

"What matters most is not the amount—it's the obedience. It's the commitment. It's the mindset that says, 'I refuse to give everything I earn to the world and leave nothing for my future.'"

I opened Scripture and reminded them of the wisdom found in **Proverbs 21:20**: *The wise have wealth and luxury, but fools spend whatever they get.*

It doesn't take a seminary degree to understand this—some of us are broke not because God didn't bless us, but because we spent every blessing as soon as it arrived.

I elaborated:

Wise people accumulate wealth because they save first.

Foolish people consume everything and are broke because they spend first.

Our communities have suffered under this pattern for generations.

We were taught survival, not stewardship.

We were taught to spend, not to save.

We were taught to look blessed instead of being blessed.

I cautioned them, "If you do not save, you are not only robbing God when you withhold the tithe—you are robbing your future, your family, and the inheritance God expects you to leave behind for your children's children."

Next, I explained the truth that every builder of wealth understands: just as you give God His tenth, you must give yourself yours. You take the first portion for the Lord, but the next portion must be set aside for your future—before the mortgage, before the light bill, before groceries, before entertainment, before anything. Because the moment you start paying yourself second, the world will find a way to take everything you have. But if you take your portion right after tithing, your money finally begins to work for you instead of you endlessly working for it.

"Start with 10 percent. If life is tight, begin with 5 percent," I advised. "The percentage is not the miracle—the discipline is. And let me tell you something I've learned over a lifetime: you will never accumulate anything by accident.

"Wealth is not the result of convenience; it is the result of conviction. If you cannot commit to saving a small amount consistently, you will never be trusted with a larger amount."

I looked at them, noting, "Some of you have never kept a financial promise to yourselves—not because you're weak, but because no one ever taught you how.

"Every time your paycheck hits, it's already spent in your mind before it even reaches your account. And that is not just bad money management—that is a violation of divine order. God requires honor first, and He requires stewardship second. You cannot keep asking Him to bless what you refuse to manage."

Then I warned them about the trap of this world: how society constantly tries to convince us to spend everything we earn. New cars, new phones, designer clothes, expensive lifestyles, impulse buys, entertainment that drains instead of builds—none of these things are wrong until they become replacements for discipline and obedience.

I pointed out, "God is not against you having nice possessions. He is against you neglecting His laws and sabotaging your future just to impress people who will forget you by next week. You cannot let temporary desires bankrupt your eternal purpose."

There is a difference between saving for emergencies and saving for destiny. One protects you from crisis; the other positions you for opportunity. When you consistently save even a small amount, something supernatural happens.

Time begins to work for you.

Discipline begins to reward you.

Your future begins to take shape.

Because money saved becomes money multiplied.

Money saved becomes seed for investments.

Money saved becomes the foundation for wealth.

And as money grows over months and years, God breathes on it—because God always blesses stewardship.

The truth every believer must understand if they want to break the cycle of financial struggle is:

"God did not give you the power to get wealth so you could die in debt.

"He did not bless you so you could leave your children nothing.

"He did not bring you this far so you could continue repeating the patterns of the past.

"It is the will of God that you steward what He places in your hands.

"That you honor Him with the tithe.

"That you honor yourself with savings.

"That you honor your family by preparing an inheritance."

I closed my Bible and said, "If you commit to this—truly commit—your life will change.

"Your mind will change.

"Your finances will change.

"Your future will change.

"Do not skip saving.

"Do not break your commitment.

"Obedience to this law will open the door to financial peace, stability, and eventually abundance."

And as I dismissed them, I told them what we would deal with next: how to protect yourself against the storms that come for every household—the storms that humility, discipline, and preparation were designed to withstand.

CHAPTER SIX

Protection against Financial Storms

By the time the next workshop session date arrived, the atmosphere had shifted inside the Empowerment Center. The room wasn't buzzing with chatter the way it usually did. Instead, there was a quiet, almost sacred heaviness in the air—like people had been left alone with their thoughts all week and were now returning with a deeper hunger. The Spiritual Law of Accumulation had done its work; it confronted them, stretched them, and forced them to face themselves. And as they settled into their seats, I could feel they were ready for what was next.

I stepped forward slowly, Bible in my hand, and looked at them with the seriousness of a man who has seen too much to sugarcoat anything. "Family, God doesn't just teach us how to honor Him with our first 10 percent and how to honor ourselves with the second. He also teaches us how to prepare for the storms of life. Because storms will come."

I let the group sit with that truth.

"You're either walking into one, walking out of one, or standing in the middle of one right now. But one thing you can count on—the storms will come."

People nodded—not because they understood the theory, but because they had lived the reality. Some had survived layoffs; others had survived sudden medical bills; still others had survived broken cars, broken seasons, and broken expectations. And I told them plainly, "Preparation is not fear. Preparation is wisdom."

Proverbs 6:6–8 offers an analogy of the ant—how it works during the summer and stores up for the winter because it knows what's coming. That's not a cute children's story. That's strategy. That is God revealing a blueprint through His creation.

The ant is God's example of self-discipline, preparation, consistency, and personal responsibility. Through the ant, God is teaching you a simple truth: save now so you don't struggle later.

I reminded them of what I'd taught the week before—how short-term savings is your emergency fund and long-term savings is your investment capital—and then I told them we were going deeper.

"Before you dream about starting a business, before you talk about buying land or investing, before you shout about generational wealth, you must build the one thing that will protect you when everything around you falls apart: an emergency fund."

And I could see people lean in because they understood instinctively that I wasn't talking about luxury—I was talking about survival.

I continued, "Storms expose whatever foundation you've been standing on. When you have an emergency fund, you don't panic when life hits you.

"You don't run to payday loans or credit cards.

"You don't start calling friends and family to bail you out.

"You face the storm with peace because you prepared for it before it arrived."

And I explained that the first assignment of that second 10 percent is protection—building a financial house strong enough to withstand the winds that come without warning using God's principles in **Matthew 7:24–27** in which Jesus makes it clear that hearing God's words alone is not enough; obedience, discipline, and truth form the unshakable foundation of a stable life.

Then I walked them through the strategy slowly, weaving the truth into their spirits. "Don't start with thousands. That's where many people quit before they even begin. Start with your first $500, which can stop a small problem from becoming a financial catastrophe. This amount can most likely fix a flat tire, repair an appliance, cover a minor medical bill, or protect your household from a crisis that would have knocked you down before.

"Stop looking for perfection and start looking for progress. Find your starting point. There's always $5 or $10 you can claim from somewhere. Cancel something you don't really need. Delay something you don't need right now. Replace a dinner out with a home-cooked meal. You don't build an emergency fund with comfort—you build it with sacrifice."

I observed someone in the front row write down the unnecessary subscriptions she was cutting. Another brother nodded as he mentally committed to cutting back on eating out. I emphasized, "It's not about the size of the sacrifice. It's about the seriousness of the commitment.

"Small sacrifices stack up.

"Small decisions shape your future.

"Small disciplines build big stability."

Then I told them something many people overlook: "Your emergency fund needs its own place, separate from your everyday spending. Separate from your swipe-and-go habits. If your emergency money is mixed with your grocery money, life will find a way for you to spend it. Put it somewhere safe, somewhere out of sight, somewhere you won't touch unless life demands it.

"And automate the savings because faith without works is dead, and savings without structure is doomed. Let the bank automatically move the money for you before you can talk yourself out of it. Don't negotiate with your future. Protect your future.

"And here's a truth that changes everything: the habit is more important than the balance. You build the first $500, then $1,000, then three months of expenses, then six. If you're married with children, you build even more. Not out of fear, but out of stewardship. Because without an emergency fund, every crisis becomes a catastrophe. But with one, every crisis becomes manageable."

I could feel the tension in the room loosen as people began to realize that financial stability was not reserved for the wealthy—it was available to the disciplined.

I stated softly but firmly, "A new pair of shoes is not a storm. A vacation is not a storm. A sale at the mall is not a storm. If the expense does not threaten your home, your health, your job, or your ability to live—it is not an emergency. Protect your fund with the same seriousness you protect your family."

Then I opened the Bible to **Luke 14:28–30**, where Jesus talks about counting the cost before building anything, and I commented on the reading. "An emergency fund is the first tower you must build in your financial city. You cannot build wealth on a shaky foundation. You cannot talk about investing while you're still drowning in crisis after crisis because you have no cushion. You cannot claim abundance while living one broken windshield away from disaster."

I stepped closer to the group and spoke as one who had survived many storms. "When you have an emergency fund, you walk differently. You breathe differently. You sleep differently. You don't live in fear anymore. You're prepared. You're steady. Your mind is clear. And you are no longer at the mercy of life."

As the workshop session came to a close, I shared a truth that I've learned over decades of ministry and financial coaching: "Building an emergency fund is not about money—it's about obedience, discipline, peace, and protection. It is the first layer of wealth. And if you build it, you will no longer be tossed around by every storm that hits."

"Amens" rose around the room—not loud, but meaningful. The kind of "Amens" that come from people who finally understand what God has been trying to teach them.

I closed my Bible and announced, "Next week, we will move into the fourth spiritual law of money—budgeting—because it doesn't matter how much God blesses you if you don't know how to direct what He puts in your hands."

THE FOURTH
SPIRITUAL LAW OF MONEY

CHAPTER SEVEN

The Spiritual Law of Budgeting

By the time the next workshop meeting arrived, the Empowerment Center again felt different—alive, expectant, almost like church right before worship breaks out. You could see it in the way people greeted each other, the way they took their seats, the way they carried themselves. What had once been a room full of uncertainty was becoming a gathering place of people who were beginning to believe—not only in God's blueprint for wealth, but in their own ability to live it. Something was shifting in them. Faith was turning into action, and hope was turning into discipline.

On a screen behind me, the Scripture for the day glowed across the room—**Haggai 1:5–6:** *Give careful thought to your ways. You have planted much, but harvested little…you earn wages, only to put them in a purse with holes in it.*

When I stepped to the front with my Bible open, I didn't sugarcoat anything. "Family, this is God speaking, not me. He's telling us to stop and think about the way we live, especially with the money He's trusted to our hands. Some of you work hard, but your bank account feels like it's leaking. You get paid, but the money disappears before you can take a breath. That's not just economics—that's spiritual misalignment."

I reminded them we were stepping into the fourth spiritual law of money—budgeting—a law that confronts one of the greatest financial traps in our community: living above the blessing.

I explained that God calls us to live according to proportional standards of our earnings. In plain words, it means don't live above your income, don't spend more than God has given you, and don't use money you don't have trying to impress people who don't care.

"Your paycheck," I said, "is not a trophy you earned—it's God's money on loan. And He will hold you accountable for how you managed it."

Then I spoke plainly, the way my elders once spoke to me. "The reason so many of our people never accumulate wealth is simple: they spend every single dollar they earn. They've been conditioned to survive, not to steward."

Proverbs 21:20 states: *The wise have wealth and luxury, but fools spend whatever they get.* That Scripture used to offend me—until I realized the Bible wasn't insulting me; it was diagnosing me.

I told them how I, too, had been that fool once. I had lived outside God's order, violated every financial principle, chased things I couldn't afford, lived for the moment, ignored my future, and drowned in the consequences.

But like the Prodigal Son, I finally saw how far I drifted when I really looked at myself one day. I saw how far I had drifted. I saw the foolishness of my choices. I saw the bondage I had created. And I said to God, "Father, I have sinned against Heaven and before You." And just like the father in the parable, God didn't shame me—He restored me. He put a robe on my shoulders, a ring on my hand, shoes on my feet, and welcomed me home. From that day forward, I owned my mistakes. I studied them. I learned from them. I became disciplined in every area of my life because I understood that discipline is the proof that faith is real.

Discipline is the path to wealth.

Discipline is the bridge between desire and destiny.

I looked at everyone in the room and stated, "Some of you are only a few feet away from everything God promised you—but you keep tripping over the same thing: lack of discipline.

"Every spiritual law we've discussed—tithing, saving, accumulation—they all collapse without discipline. This law is where the shift happens. Because budgeting is the tool God uses to teach you self-control."

Then I shared why so many believers struggle. Budgets force you to confront your habits. Budgets reveal every hidden leak, every unnecessary purchase, every emotional decision, every late-night impulse buy you justified as a "reward." People hate budgets, not because budgets are hard, but because they expose truth. But without one, you will always feel like you have "more month than money." Budgeting is not bondage—it is freedom. It is you telling your money where to go instead of wondering where it went.

I reminded the group that even billionaires cannot satisfy every desire. Desire grows like a weed—faster than your income, faster than your discipline, faster than your wisdom—unless you learn how to pull it up by the roots. God is not against you enjoying life. He is against you bankrupting your destiny trying to satisfy desires that were never meant to rule you. Jesus made it plain in **Luke 16:10** when He said: *if you cannot be trusted with little, you will not be trusted with* *much.* God will never give you what you have already demonstrated you cannot manage.

Then I shifted from Scripture to spirit. "The Spiritual Law of Budgeting has one goal: to teach you how to live within your means, honor God first, honor yourself second, and eliminate the financial burdens that keep you enslaved.

"God does not call His children to live in constant stress. He calls us to order. To stewardship. To wisdom. To balance. And if you live by His order—tithing first, saving second, living third—your household will experience peace instead of financial panic."

I spoke to everyone like a father because that's what some of them needed. I told them to look at their spending for the last thirty days. Not with guilt, not with fear, but with honesty.

"Your bank statement," I said, "is a spiritual document. It will reveal what you value. It will show you what controls you. If you want to know where your heart is, follow your money."

I explained how so many families lose wealth not through catastrophes, but through small, undisciplined habits—too much eating out, too many subscriptions, too much convenience spending, too much impulse buying. Every small decision becomes a silent thief.

I spoke about the dangers of debt—not to shame them, but to free them—saying, "Debt is the world's counterfeit version of God's provision." It gives you what you want today in exchange for your tomorrow. That's why **Romans 13:8** tells us: *owe no man anything.*

"Debt robs you of peace.

"Debt steals your seed.

"Debt hijacks your future before you even reach it."

As I continued, the room grew still. People weren't discouraged—but determined. They were seeing themselves clearly for the first time. They were seeing their patterns, their blind spots, their excuses. And they were realizing that budgeting wasn't punishment—it was alignment.

I talked about something I had learned over the years. "When you budget, you take authority over your life. You reclaim control. You silence chaos. You say to your money, 'You will not decide my future—I will.' And when you give careful thought to your ways, as God commands, you will walk in the kind of wisdom that Heaven honors."

Before I closed the workshop session, I looked around the room and then spoke, "Family, a budget is not about *restriction*—it is about *direction*. If you do not direct your money, the world will. And trust me—the world has no interest in you being financially free."

The room sat in quiet wonder, and for the first time in a long time, I could feel that people weren't just listening—they were surrendering. They were ready.

CHAPTER EIGHT

The Habits of Discipline and Self-Control

The workshop attendees in the Empowerment Center were unusually quiet for this session, the kind of quiet that only settles over a room when people know something real is about to be revealed. I walked to the front with my Bible in hand and took a moment to scan their faces—people who had been coming week after week, people who had started to believe in the possibility of change, people who were beginning to trust God's blueprint more than their old behaviors. And I asked the question I knew every person had wrestled with:

"Who here has ever looked at their bank account and asked, 'where did all my money go?'"

The entire room burst into knowing laughter with hands shooting up everywhere and sighs spilling out like confessions. That's when I smiled, not because their struggle was funny but because the honesty was finally breaking through.

"Family," I said gently, "that question—that feeling—is the evidence of the consumer mindset at work.

"The consumer reacts to desires.

"The consumer spends first and thinks later.

"The consumer chases the moment and ignores the consequences.

"But God never called you to be consumers—He called you to be stewards of what He has entrusted to you."

I walked to the white board and wrote two truths that hung in the room like a spiritual diagnosis:

The consumer spends first.

The steward budgets first.

I told them how the world conditions us to believe that if we want something, we deserve it immediately. Companies make billions manufacturing urgency—flash sales, limited-time offers, last-chance deals—hoping you'll mistake emotional desire for need. And yet God's Word has been instructing us for thousands of years: *The wise store up, but fools devour everything.* I let that Scripture in **Proverbs 21:20** linger because it exposes a painful truth many don't want to face—wisdom saves, but foolishness spends.

What does a steward actually do? A steward flips the order. A steward puts needs before wants, purpose before impulse, and planning before pleasure. A steward understands that God blesses order—and when you manage the little with care, God can trust you with more. Discipline and self-control are the two habits that transform a spender into a steward, and both of them will challenge everything in you that wants the easy way out.

Discipline is the quiet strength that helps you stay committed to your financial destiny even when everything around you is calling your name. Discipline is waking up with a plan instead of living by impulse. Discipline is telling your money where to go before it slips through your fingers. I reminded the group that discipline is never supposed to feel good at first; Scripture tells us it's often painful. But later—always later—it produces a harvest of peace.

We then talked about the twin companion of discipline—self-control.

Self-control is the power to say no right now so you can say yes later. It is the strength to walk past a sale and keep your money in your pocket. It is the voice that whispers, "Don't buy it—you don't need it." It is the protection that keeps the enemy from invading your life through impulse."

I read aloud **Proverbs 25:28**: *A person without self-control is like a city with broken-down walls.* And I plainly told the group, "If you don't build your walls, the world will spend your money for you. Every advertisement, every craving, every emotion will invade your finances."

I could see the room change as those words landed. People sat straighter, eyes became sharper and hearts, softer. They were starting to realize that the real battle wasn't outside of them—it was inside. I told them, "When you embrace discipline and self-control, you shift from being a consumer who reacts to life, into a steward who directs life. You stop being led by impulses and start being led by purpose."

Then came the testimonies—raw, honest, transforming....

Tasha, a single mother of two, stood first and with courage in her voice spoke about how she used to spend money as fast as she earned it. She believed any extra money meant she had the right to indulge immediately. But it wasn't freedom—it was bondage disguised as pleasure. She told the others how she challenged herself not to buy anything outside her budget for 30 days—and that one act of discipline allowed her to pay off a credit card in two months. She said she finally felt free.

Then young Laila shared her story, her voice steady but humbled. She confessed that she once believed her financial struggle came from not earning enough. But when she tracked her spending, she saw the truth—hundreds of dollars wasted on eating out, clothes she didn't need, impulse buys she couldn't even remember. She changed her habits, saved 15 percent of her income, and started making choices aligned with purpose instead of emotion. She said she felt in control for the first time in her life.

And next, Anthony, a retired military brother, expressed his former situation with a calmness in his eyes that only comes when a man tells the truth about himself. He said how, even with a pension, he was living check to check because he couldn't say no to his wants—boats, gadgets, trips, toys. But when he embraced budgeting as a spiritual discipline, he realized his wants had been stealing from his future. He stood there debt-free for the first time since his twenties, a living witness to the power of order.

I looked around the room, watching those testimonies sink into the hearts of everyone listening, and I offered, "Family, hear me clearly—the Spiritual Law of Budgeting is not about money. It's about stewardship. God is watching to see how you manage what He has already placed in your hands. Discipline and self-control are the two guardrails that will protect you from drifting into financial disaster.

"Without discipline, you'll repeat old patterns.

"Without self-control, your desires will outrun your destiny.

"But with both—you'll have more than enough to save, invest, and bless others."

I paused, letting the weight of the message settle into the soul of each in the room.

"You are not consumers," I told them. "You are Kingdom stewards. Every decision you make with your money either brings you closer to freedom or deeper into bondage. So, draw a line today. Declare that you will no longer live at the mercy of your impulses. You will master your money, so your money no longer masters you."

And with a warm, knowing smile, I ended the workshop session with, "Next week, we step into the fifth spiritual law of money—intentionality—and we're going to deal with something many believers avoid: the connection among debt, spiritual bondage, and God's blueprint for freedom."

THE FIFTH
SPIRITUAL LAW OF MONEY

CHAPTER NINE

The Spiritual Law of Intentionality

The room at the Empowerment Center had a reverent silence this session, the kind that settles when people sense they are about to confront something they have avoided for too long. I stepped forward with my Bible in hand, not to lecture them, but to deliver a truth that has crippled generations and kept God's people from walking in the fullness of their freedom. My voice was calm, but it carried the weight of authority that comes from both Scripture and experience.

"Family," I began quietly, "before we can move any further in this financial journey, we must confront one of the greatest enemies of both your wealth and your spiritual walk—debt."

I let that word linger in the air because I could see the discomfort rise in their faces.

"Debt is not just a financial issue; it is a spiritual one. And if you do not learn to make decisions intentionally—on purpose, with purpose, and by God's purpose, you will spend your life bound to something God never ordained for you."

I continued speaking, sharing my experience. Scripture never condemns borrowing, but it does command wisdom. Jesus Himself said in **Luke 14:28** that before a man builds anything, he must *sit down and calculate the cost to see whether he can finish it.*

God is not against you building a life, buying a home, or making wise investments. But He is against you stepping into obligations without prayer, without planning, without clarity, and without counting the cost. Debt taken without intention becomes bondage disguised as opportunity.

Proverbs 22:7 warns that "the borrower becomes a slave to the lender," pointing out that slavery did not end in 1865, it just changed forms.

Today, slavery shows up as interest rates, monthly payments, late fees, and fine print.

It shows up through credit cards designed to keep you dependent.

It shows up through car loans that rob you of financial oxygen.

It shows up through student loans that crush dreams before they even begin.

Debt is a master many serve faithfully without ever realizing they have bowed their knee.

Then I softened my tone because I knew I was speaking from a place many of them had lived. "Debt will steal your peace. Debt will occupy your mind. Debt will hijack your prayers. Debt will make you doubt whether God is speaking, when in reality, you are simply too overwhelmed to hear Him."

I spoke about believers who felt God calling them into ministry, but their loans kept them chained to a job. Parents who wanted to start a business but were shackled by credit cards. Families who longed to give generously but were imprisoned by car notes and payday loans. Debt narrows your world until all you can see is obligation and survival.

The only way out of this slavery to debt is intentionality. Not desperation, not wishful thinking, not hoping the problem will disappear, but a Spirit-led decision to honor God with your plans and obey Him with your actions.

The Spiritual Law of Intentionality turns you from a passive victim of your circumstances into an active steward of God's resources. When you decide to address your debt with purpose, something shifts. Heaven responds to order. God honors clarity. The Holy Spirit strengthens discipline. And progress, even slow progress, becomes a testimony.

Many believers use one of two approaches to attack debt—one that gives quick wins and builds momentum (Debt Snowball Method) and the other that saves the most money over time (Debt Avalanche Method). I did not present these approaches as formulas. Instead, I presented them as strategies that require prayer, patience, and discipline. Because at the end of the day, it is not the method that frees you; it is the mindset. What matters is that you start somewhere and refuse to quit.

Then I gave them each a debt destruction worksheet—listing type of debt, total balance, interest rate, and minimum payment—to record their personal debt. I watched people in the room shift uncomfortably as they finally saw, on paper, in black and white, the weight they had been carrying in their spirits. Then I gently reminded them, "Tonight is not about shame. Tonight is about intention."

DEBT DESTRUCTION WORKSHEET

Type of Debt	Total Balance	Interest Rate	Minimum Payment
Credit Card	$ 1,200	24.9%	$ 45
Credit Card	$ 500	21.0%	$ 25
Personal Loan	$ 2,500	19.0 %	$ 95
Auto Loan	$11,800	6.0%	$385
Student Loan	$18,400	5.5%	$150

I asked them to pray over their lists, not with fear but with expectation. To ask God for guidance, for discipline, for unexpected provision, for supernatural acceleration—but to also remember that God blesses what you commit to Him, not what you ignore.

And then the individual testimonies began.

Sister Angela stood and shared how she once carried $15,000 in credit card debt—15,000 pounds of shame, anxiety, and spiritual heaviness. She listed the debt and how she used the Debt Snowball Method to become debt-free.

Card	Balance	Interest
Credit Card 1	$ 1,200	10%
Credit Card 2	$ 2,300	17%
Credit Card 3	$ 4,000	12%
Credit Card 4	$ 7,500	7%
Total Debt	$15,000	

She said this list felt like confession—honest, uncomfortable, but freeing.

Each month, she paid the **minimum** on all cards *except* the smallest balance.

That $1,200 credit card became her focus.

She prayed before every payment.

"Every dollar felt like a small deliverance," she said. "I wasn't just paying debt—I was releasing bondage."

When the $1,200 credit card was paid off, something shifted.

- One bill disappeared.
- One burden lifted.
- One victory recorded.

The payment she had been making on that card didn't disappear—it **rolled forward**.

Now, she attacked the $2,300 credit card with:

- Its regular payment.
- PLUS the payment from the paid-off card.

Momentum replaced discouragement. With each debt paid off, her "snowball" grew larger:

- $1,200 gone → confidence
- $2,300 gone → hope
- $4,000 gone → discipline strengthened
- $7,500 gone → freedom within reach

She said the method worked not just because of math—but because **small wins healed her mindset**. Two years later, when the last payment was made, she spoke of the peace that came with it as though she had rediscovered her breath.

Brother Marcus then shared how he took control of his finances by targeting the debt that was costing him the most in interest. By staying focused and disciplined, he eliminated that burden and freed up an extra $600 each month—money that no longer paid for past mistakes but now moved him closer to the future he was intentionally building.

When everyone finished sharing their situation, I looked around that room and felt a wave of hope rise in me. These weren't stories of theory; they were stories of transformation. Stories of people who had once been buried under debt but were now stepping into freedom because they chose to live intentionally.

So, I closed with the truth the Spirit pressed on my heart.

"The Spiritual Law of Intentionality is about doing things on purpose, for a purpose, with God's purpose in mind. Debt wants to dictate your life. Debt wants to tell you what you can give, where you can go, what you can sacrifice, what you can dream.

"But God did not create you to serve lenders. He created you to serve Him."

I lifted my eyes and looked around the room, noting, "You cannot serve two masters. And tonight, you must choose whom you want directing your life—your debt or your God."

The room grew still, almost holy, as the weight of that choice settled on each heart.

I concluded the workshop session with, "Next week, I'll show you how determination and persistence will carry you through this journey when your emotions, your fear, and the enemy try to pull you back into bondage.

"But, for now. Sit with God. Let Him reveal the next step. And be intentional about your decision."

CHAPTER TEN

The Habits of Determination and Persistence

The meeting in the Empowerment Center this session was unusually quiet, the kind of quiet that comes when people are no longer in denial about where they are—and are finally ready to confront what it will take to get where God is calling them. Determination hung in the air like incense. When I stepped to the front of the room, Bible in one hand, marker in the other, I could feel the weight of their expectations. They were ready, not for a lecture, but for truth—the kind that doesn't just inform you but transforms you.

"Family," I began, waiting for everyone to settle and listen, "getting out of debt is not just about numbers. It is not simply about interest rates, balances, and payoff dates. Getting out of debt is about mindset. And your mindset must be shaped by two spiritual habits most people rarely talk about: determination and persistence.

"Because the greatest enemy to your financial freedom is not lack of money—it is discouragement. And discouragement will visit you every time progress feels slow."

I opened the Scriptures to **Proverbs 6** and read about the ant—small, unnoticed, uncelebrated, yet unstoppable. "Look at this creature," I directed them. "It works with focus, discipline, determination, and persistence.

No one is clapping for it.

No one is rewarding it.

No one is prescribing a plan for it.

Yet it keeps moving with purpose because its survival—and its future—depend on it."

I paused and added, "That is intentionality. That is the spiritual law we have been learning. But intentionality is powerless without determination to nourish it and persistence to sustain it."

I continued to explain. Having a plan is only the beginning. Many people write a debt destruction plan with excitement, but excitement doesn't last. Progress slows. Life happens. Emergencies arise. Temptations whisper. Old habits return with familiar voices. And the moment progress stops feeling dramatic, most people stop altogether.

That is why the Spirit insists that determination must anchor you.

Determination is the quiet, inner decision that says, "I refuse to stay in bondage. I refuse to serve debt for the rest of my life. I refuse to bow down to payments that rob my peace, my joy, and my purpose."

Determination is the voice inside that rises up when everything around you tells you to quit. It is the spiritual backbone that whispers "Keep going. God did not bring you this far for you to surrender now." But determination alone cannot carry you across the finish line.

Determination is the fire that starts the journey; persistence is the discipline that finishes it.

Persistence is not loud. It is not glamorous.

Persistence is not emotional.

Persistence is a daily decision.

Persistence is making a payment when you would rather make a purchase.

Persistence is honoring your budget when everything in you wants a moment of escape.

Persistence is choosing long-term peace over short-term pleasure.

Persistence is the quiet, spiritual muscle that grows every time you refuse to turn back.

I cautioned them, "Debt freedom is not a sprint. It is a pilgrimage. You walk out of bondage the same way Israel walked out of Egypt—step by step, day by day, with God's guidance and your obedience working hand in hand."

I further explained my thinking. When determination fuels your why and persistence shapes your how, something supernatural begins to happen.

Your mind becomes clearer.

Your priorities become sharper.

Your spending becomes more purposeful.

Your temptations lose their grip.

Your victories—no matter how small—start to accumulate.

And God, seeing your faithfulness, begins to accelerate the process in ways you could not have orchestrated on your own.

I looked around the room and spoke the truth no one likes hearing but everyone needs:

"There will be days when you don't feel like trying. Days when you ask yourself if it's even worth it. Days when the progress feels microscopic. Days when you want to compromise or slip back into old habits. But hear me—your freedom depends on your persistence. Every payment is a declaration of faith. Every sacrifice is a seed. Every step forward is an act of spiritual warfare. The enemy wants you in debt because debt distracts you, depresses you, and delays you. But God wants you free."

I could feel the room leaning in as I continued. "Persistence is not about perfection. It's about direction. As long as you keep moving forward, as long as you keep refusing to quit, as long as you keep honoring the plan God has given you, you will win. Not because you are strong, but because you are steadfast. And steadfastness always produces victory."

I reminded them of the testimonies from the previous week—the sister who paid off $15,000 in credit card debt through patience and prayer, the brother who freed up $600 a month through discipline and consistency. Their breakthroughs did not come from sudden miracles but from daily choices, small victories compounded over time.

Determination kept their hope alive.

Persistence kept their feet moving.

As we drew closer to ending the workshop session, I shared what the Spirit pressed into my heart.

"God honors a steward who refuses to surrender. He honors the one who chooses obedience over impulse. He honors the one who says, 'Lord, I will trust You even when progress is slow.' And He honors the one who holds their course with persistence until every chain is broken."

The room was silent, but it was not the silence of people's confusion—it was the silence of their conviction. They knew what God was requiring of them. They understood now that debt freedom would require more than a plan. It would require a posture—a spiritual posture of endurance and unwavering commitment.

I closed by saying, "Family, as you walk out these doors tonight, understand this: your debt will not disappear overnight, but your bondage can. Because bondage ends the moment you decide to fight. And when determination takes hold of your heart and persistence takes hold of your habits, freedom becomes inevitable."

I smiled as I concluded the evening's meeting, knowing the next chapter would push them even deeper into God's financial blueprint.

"Next week," I said, "we step into the sixth spiritual law of money—sowing and reaping. It will challenge how you view increase and prepare your spirit to handle blessing before it arrives. Come ready. What we cover next may change the way you receive from God for the rest of your life."

THE SIXTH
SPIRITUAL LAW OF MONEY

CHAPTER ELEVEN

The Spiritual Law of Sowing and Reaping

The atmosphere in the Empowerment Center's room carried a different kind of weight as the workshop started. I heard the sound of people who had tasted progress and wanted more. They had cut unnecessary spending. They had built their first savings accounts. Some had started side hustles or resurrected forgotten ideas to earn money. They had begun to understand that wealth wasn't just a dream—it was a process. And now they stood at the doorway of a deeper truth: money is not meant to sit still. It is meant to move, multiply, and manifest God's purpose. They were ready for the next step.

I stepped forward with my Bible in hand, watching their faces as they leaned forward, hungry for revelation.

"Family," I began, "tonight we enter into a law that governs every blessing God releases—whether it's spiritual, emotional, or financial. It is the spiritual law that determines your harvest. It is the law that separates those who accumulate from those who multiply. It is the Spiritual Law of Sowing and Reaping."

I opened the Scriptures to **Luke 19:12–13**, where Jesus tells the story of a nobleman who gave silver to his servants before leaving for a distant land. *"Invest this for me while I am gone,"* I read, letting the words echo through the room.

"Not spend it. Not bury it. Not protect it in fear. Invest it. Put it to work. Multiply it. Grow what God gave you."

I looked around the room before continuing my point.

"Family, this parable is not about church work.

"It is about wealth.

"It is about investment.

"It is about stewardship.

"It is about responsibility.

"It is about accountability.

"It is about economics.

"It is about the Kingdom mandate placed on every believer to increase—spiritually, mentally, emotionally, physically, and financially. What you have in your hands is not meant to die in a bank account. God didn't give you gifts, skills, savings, or ideas so they could remain unused. He gave them to you to sow because nothing multiplies until it is planted."

But before we moved on to discuss sowing money into investments, I told them the truth many people overlook:

"Your first act of sowing is always into the Kingdom of God. Why? Because God refuses to bless financial disobedience. You cannot ask Him to multiply money that you refuse to honor Him with."

I reminded them that the Kingdom isn't limited to the four walls of a sanctuary.

"The Kingdom," I said, "is everywhere God's will is being done—your nonprofits, your schools, your community programs, your land, your businesses. The Earth is the

Lord's. Every resource belongs to Him. And He expects His children to steward it."

I turned to **Genesis 26:12** and read about Isaac planting in famine and reaping one hundredfold in the same year. That wasn't a financial miracle—it was a spiritual principle of sowing in faith, and being obedient despite the economic conditions.

When you plant in obedience, you reap under God's favor. When you bury your seed, you bury your future. When Jesus said the good soil produces thirty-, sixty-, and a hundredfold returns, He was revealing the supernatural potential of a seed placed in the right environment.

I looked at the group and asked, "Do you understand what this means? Your money is a seed. Your gifts are a seed. Your time is a seed. Your discipline is a seed. And God will only multiply what you sow."

Then I shared something deeper—something our ancestors knew instinctively but the modern world trained us to forget: collective wealth is Kingdom wealth.

"What if we pooled our resources the way our ancestors did when they built Black Wall Street?" I asked.

"What if we used our gifts, labor, and money not just for our individual lives, but to build something that would outlive us?

"What if we bought land together, started businesses together, opened schools, clinics, factories?

"What if we stopped asking systems designed to limit us for permission to rise?"

I saw fire light up in their eyes. They could see it—a community rising not through charity but through ownership.

"Imagine," I said, "that every time you shop, you are supporting a business owned by the community. Imagine profits flowing back into families, neighborhoods, and ministries. That is how you break poverty. That is how you build power. That is how you rebuild a people."

But I also reminded them that planting requires wisdom. Not every investment is good soil. "If it sounds too good to be true, it is," I said simply. "God does not bless shortcuts to wealth. He blesses the faithful. He blesses the diligent. He blesses the ones who test the spirit before they sign the contract, who research before they buy land, who pray before they invest in a business partnership."

I then noted:

"Greed will whisper.

"Deception will disguise itself as opportunity.

"But discernment is your protection."

As I continued speaking, I watched their faces shift from excitement to conviction to revelation. They were beginning to understand that wealth is not an accident. It is not luck. It is not a miracle without responsibility. Wealth is the harvest of seeds sown with intention, patience, and faith.

"Family, God is watching how you handle what He has already placed in your hands. If you bury it, you lose it. If you hoard it, it withers. But if you sow it, if you multiply it, if you use it to bless His Kingdom and your community, He will increase you beyond your imagination."

I let the words settle and closed the workshop session with this truth:

"You reap what you sow. Not what you wish for. Not what you dream about. Not what you pray for without action. You reap what you sow. And, in God's Kingdom, the harvest always exceeds the seed."

They left the Empowerment Center buzzing—dreaming of land, businesses, investment groups, and legacies. Some were already forming quiet partnerships. Others were imagining what their savings could become over time.

All of them walked away with the same truth burning in their hearts:

A planted seed is a future already written.

A buried seed is a future surrendered.

And the moment you begin to sow on purpose—your harvest becomes inevitable.

CHAPTER TWELVE

The Habits of Patience and Diligence

There was a quiet stillness in the Empowerment Center's room for this workshop session—a kind of sacred hush that only comes when people feel destiny drawing near. The room had shifted over the weeks. People who once walked in timid, skeptical, or ashamed of their past financial mistakes now carried notebooks filled with strategies, testimonies, and small victories. Some had paid down debt. Some had created savings accounts for the first time in their lives. Some were learning how to multiply what they had. And all of them were beginning to believe not just in principles, but in themselves.

I stood at the front of the room with my Bible in one hand and a tiny seed packet in the other. I looked at the packet, then looked into their faces. "This," I began, taking out a seed and lifting it between my fingers, "is a promise. But a promise without cultivation will never become anything more than potential."

I let the words linger in the silence before unfolding the Scriptures.

I read again from **Genesis 26:12** where Isaac sowed in famine, reaping a hundredfold, becoming wealthy in a land that was barren.

"Family, Isaac didn't reap because the soil was good—he reaped because God blessed him. But hear me—Isaac still had to plant. He still had to wait. The blessing accelerated his harvest, but not before obedience planted the seed."

I told them something most people don't want to accept: "God's blessing does not eliminate the process, it accelerates what the process was already producing. Isaac didn't see a harvest because he wished for it. He saw it because he sowed for it. And then he stayed in the land long enough for God to do what only God can do."

I turned to the white board and wrote two words:

Patience

Diligence

"These," I said, pointing to the words, "are the two habits most believers despise, but they are the very habits that determine whether your seed ever becomes anything more than a dream."

I explained *patience*—not the passive sitting and waiting kind, but the spiritual posture that refuses to uproot what God is growing just because it isn't happening on your timetable. Patience is the ability to trust God's timing even when nothing seems to be happening. It guards you from panic, from comparison, from desperate decisions. It is knowing that God may be working underground, unseen, while you are tempted to call your seed a failure.

Then I explained *diligence*. If patience guards you from uprooting your seed, diligence keeps you from starving it.

"Diligence," I told them, "is showing up when nothing is moving.

"It is watering when you don't see sprouting.

"It is budgeting when your savings looks small.

"It is sowing even when you feel like your harvest is far.

"Diligence is the labor of faith—the steady hand that refuses to abandon the field just because the fruit isn't visible yet."

I looked around the room and spoke in a low voice, "Without patience, you will abandon your seed before it matures. Without diligence, you will neglect your seed and then it dies. But when patience and diligence meet, harvest is inevitable—because God blesses both faithfulness in work and faithfulness in waiting."

Next I shared a story.

"Some of you know Sister Lorraine," I said. "Two years ago, she sat in this room unsure if she could ever see real change. She took $10 here, $20 there—and she started saving. She joined a few sisters in this workshop to invest together. Some months she wanted to quit. Some months she thought the money was too slow. But she stayed. She kept planting and nurturing. She kept building. She kept showing up—even when nothing was happening. Then, last year, that group purchased a small parcel of land on the outskirts of town. Two months ago—without doing anything but holding it—that land doubled in value."

The room murmured. Some shook their heads in amazement.

"That," I said, once again lifting the seed, "is what happens when patience meets diligence—God steps in and breathes on what your hands have tended."

Then I leaned forward, my voice shifting from narrative to confrontation. "But let's be honest—most people will never see the harvest God intended because they lack patience. They abort their blessings because waiting feels like waste.

They tear up their own soil because they cannot stand the feeling of slow progress. And so, they sabotage themselves—not because they lacked opportunity, but because they lacked endurance."

I reminded them that Scripture never promised instant harvests. **Ecclesiastes 3:1–2** posits *there is a time to plant and a time to harvest*—but it never says those times are close together. "That space in between," I continued, "is the wilderness where God trains you, purifies you, matures you, and prepares you to handle what you asked for."

Here is the truth: God will never give you a harvest you don't have the discipline to manage. "Some blessings are delayed," I said, "not because God said no—but because you are not yet strong enough to carry the yes."

The room went still. Then I said the words that most people avoid: "Growth requires waiting. Waiting requires faith. And faith requires work.

"Some of you came tonight ready to walk away from your budget, your business plan, your investment partnership, your debt reduction journey—not because it isn't working, but because it isn't working fast enough. Let me speak prophetically—your soil is fine. Your seed is still alive. You are simply in the season where patience must do what force cannot."

I lifted the seed yet again, saying. "This has everything it needs to grow except someone willing to plant it and someone willing to wait."

And finally, I shared what every believer needs to hear before they quit on their own harvest: "Do not dig up in doubt what you planted in faith."

I reminded them of Abraham—who waited decades for a son; of Joseph—who waited years in prison before command; of David—anointed as king but sent back to tend sheep; of Moses—wandering forty years before deliverance; of Israel—waiting generations for a promise. "God makes you grow before He lets your harvest grow," I said softly. "Because what God gives you will always match who you have become."

People's body posture shifted. Eyes softened. Hands loosened. A few even wiped tears. I closed my Bible and spoke from that space between spirit and instruction:

"Family, if you plant faithfully, work faithfully, and wait faithfully—your harvest is guaranteed. It will not come when you want it. It will not look how you imagined it. But it will come—pressed down, shaken together, and running over—because diligent hands and patient hearts never go unrewarded in the Kingdom."

I let the words settle like morning dew on a meadow.

"Tonight," I suggested, "I want you to walk away with something greater than information. I want you to walk away with endurance. Hold your ground. Water your vision. Protect your seed. And, for God's sake, stop comparing your season to someone else's harvest. You don't know how long they waited, how long they labored, how many tears they sowed. Run your race. Work your field. Trust your God."

The room went silent—not with emptiness, but with revelation. I concluded the workshop session with:

"Patience is faith stretched through time.

"Diligence is faith expressed through work.

"When you join them, your seed can do nothing but grow."

I smiled seeing how people were awakening. "Next week," I announced, "we will step into the seventh spiritual law of money—manifestation—because when you obey God's wealth-building laws, your life reflects His blessing."

THE SEVENTH
SPIRITUAL LAW OF MONEY

CHAPTER THIRTEEN

The Spiritual Law of Manifestation

I felt something electric in the atmosphere at the Empowerment Center—not loud, not flashy, but subtle, like the quiet trembling of leaves before rain breaks open the clouds. People were leaning forward more now. They weren't just attending a workshop anymore—they were waiting for God to say something about the future they had finally started believing belonged to them. I stepped forward with my Bible in hand, not as a lecturer, but as a witness who had seen what happens when broken people begin to align their lives with divine law. I did not open with numbers, budgets, or strategies. I opened with a declaration.

"Family, God has already appointed blessings with your name on them, but He will not release them until He knows you're ready to receive."

The people in the room shifted. Hands lifted. Heads bowed. Someone whispered, "Yes, Lord." You could feel the ache, and the hunger of people who have survived lack, but never learned how to live in overflow. Some of them didn't just want a principle, they needed a breakthrough. And I told them the truth: the blessing isn't waiting on God. God is waiting on you.

I began naming the invisible chains. The ones that stalk Black households generation after generation.

Scarcity thinking.

Financial trauma.

Silent inferiority.

Learned helplessness passed down like dysfunctional inheritance.

"For too long," I said, "we have been conditioned to believe that wealth belonged to other people and that we should be grateful just to survive." But the God of Scripture does not speak survival, He speaks abundance.

Israel did not leave Egypt with just enough, they left with gold, silver, livestock, and favor.

Jesus did not feed the five thousand with barely enough. He produced overflow, with left over baskets.

Paul did not tell the Philippians God would meet a few needs, he said all needs, according to His riches, not according to their trauma.

"But here is the enemy's strategy," I told them. "He knows he cannot stop God from blessing you, so he tries to stop you from believing you deserve the blessing."

Scarcity is not merely economic—it is spiritual warfare. It robs your identity before it robs your bank account. It convinces you that increase is suspicious, favor is temporary, and overflow is reserved for someone else.

Then I read **Philippians 4:19** aloud. Slowly, like a courtroom verdict: *And my God will supply all your needs according to His riches in glory.*

I said to the group, "*Riches* is not symbolic. God's glory is not poverty. Heaven has no budget crisis. The Spiritual Law of Manifestation teaches that when your faith, words, habits, and posture align with God's intentions, what He ordained begins to appear in your life."

I reminded them that the previous spiritual laws of money—acquisition, tithing, accumulation, budgeting, intentionality, and sowing and reaping—were not random. They were formation. They were pruning. They were spiritual training.

"You cannot manifest a harvest you have not matured enough to handle," I said. "God does not reward desire; He rewards stewardship."

Then I gave them the analogy Heaven had given me: God treats promotion the way an employer treats hiring. "Your interview was believing God could bless you. Your training was applying the laws. Your manifestation is Heaven saying, 'They're ready—release it.'"

I moved from proclamation to preparation because blessing without readiness becomes burden. I noted, "You cannot pray for blessings you haven't prepared for.

"Expectation without structure is fantasy.

"Structure without expectation is religion.

"But when expectation and structure meet—manifestation begins."

I guided them through dismantling limiting beliefs by explaining the lies they inherited from lack, and replacing them with the truths God had been speaking for generations:

"I am worthy of wealth because I am my Father's child."

"Money flows to me according to God's design."

"God's supply is endless—therefore my life will not remain empty."

I told them to write their Blessing Blueprint—a plan for how they would honor God with whatever increase came their way.

"If God gave you $100,000 today, and you don't know what to do with it," I said, "that is proof you are not ready. Heaven does not release to unprepared hands."

I had them speak the following declaration every morning for twenty-one days—not because repetition is magic, but because faith that is not spoken stays imprisoned in the mind.

"Heaven moves when earth agrees."

I said, "You must hear yourself say what God has been trying to convince you to believe."

I instructed them to perform acts of faith—small actions that signaled expectation: opening a second savings account, separating business money from personal money, organizing old bills, creating a giving envelope, cleaning a corner of their house to make room for new things.

"Faith isn't loud," I told them. "Faith organizes."

Then testimonies began pouring in like light breaking through curtained windows.

Angela's unexpected bonus.

Marcus' unexpected business contract.

DeShawn's unclaimed check—provision he didn't even know was his.

I showed them what was really happening: obedience had become alignment—and alignment had become attraction.

"Manifestation," I declared, "is not God changing His mind—it is you finally becoming who He always said you were."

I spoke slowly now because revelation needs stillness to land.

"God does not send blessings to impress you. He sends them because you have proven you will steward them, multiply them, and return them to His purposes."

I closed my Bible and spoke what I knew Heaven wanted them to hear:

"Blessings do not get lost. They do not wander. They do not forget addresses. They come when the heart, the habits, the posture, and the assignment align."

I looked into faces that were no longer merely hopeful, but awakened. "Next week," I said, "we will step into the eighth spiritual law of money—purpose—because manifestation without mission becomes pride. God does not bless you so you can shine, He blesses you so you can build."

And as they gathered their belongings, I saw a change in them. People walked differently. They did not leave as financial students, they left as deserving heirs.

Because manifestation is not a season, it is an identity.

THE EIGHTH
SPIRITUAL LAW OF MONEY

CHAPTER FOURTEEN

Spiritual Law of Purpose

By the time this session started in the Empowerment Center, the room no longer felt like a workshop; it felt like the birthing floor of destiny. People walked in with notebooks ready, hearts open, eyes burning with newfound expectation. They weren't merely learning principles anymore, they were beginning to recognize calling. I stood at the front, Bible open, and I didn't begin with numbers or strategies. I began with truth.

"Family," I said, "money is not paper. It is assignment stamped in ink. It is not wealth for wealth's sake; it is divine equipment."

I let the workshop attendees sit in that.

Some people had never heard money described as holy. They had heard sermons about stewardship, warnings about greed, rebukes for lack, but very few had ever been told that wealth is ministry. So, I said it again:

"God gives wealth because God gives work."

I told them the Spiritual Law of Purpose is the thread that ties all the others together. You can acquire money by the power God gives. You can manifest blessings. You can multiply seed. But without purpose, you become a wealthy prodigal son or daughter wandering without assignment, owning resources but lacking direction.

"Purpose," I said, "is what keeps blessing from becoming idolatry.

"Purpose is the difference between stewardship and self-indulgence, between empire-building and Kingdom-building."

I reminded them of the Law of Acquisition and that God whispers blueprints through ideas, gifts, skills, and visions.

"When God places a business idea in you," I pointed out, "He is not thinking about Gucci, Prada, Coach, Michael Kors, or Valentino; he is thinking about generational assignment. God does not fund ego. He funds missions."

I wrote the progression on the white board so they could see the unfolding:

Gift → Skill → Purpose → Provision → Impact

"This is Heaven's supply chain. God will never send provision where purpose has not been acknowledged."

I began speaking in a voice of giving testimony, not dispensing theory. "Money is meant to bless your house, yes. But it is also meant to heal trauma, rebuild systems, restore dignity, repair neighborhoods, raise children who never taste lack, and lift the poor from dependence into destiny."

Then I read **Matthew 25:35–36**—not the parable of talents this time, but the parable of compassion. *For I was hungry…thirsty…a stranger….* "This passage is not merely about meeting needs, it is about restoring honor to those the world has broken.

"Feeding the hungry is the first gesture," I continued. "But feeding them once and leaving them starving again is not Kingdom. Teaching people to feed themselves, that is Kingdom. Giving them tools, access, and opportunity; that is

Kingdom. Showing them their worth so they do not shrink back into dependence; that is Kingdom."

I spoke about the storehouse, not as a building but as a mission station.

"You cannot tithe into dead soil," I told them. "If your church or nonprofit is only building walls while the community outside is financially drowning, that storehouse is misaligned with the Word of God. Because God never told the Church to build monuments, He told it to build people."

I shared the proverb many people quote: *Give a man a fish, feed him a day; teach a man to fish, feed him for life.* Then I rephrased it the way Heaven taught it to me: "Give a man a fishing rod, teach him how to use it, and remind him the King of kings owns the lake."

That revelation really hit people in the room because it shifted their identity. "You are not beggars," I told them. "You are heirs who forgot your Father's estate."

Then I turned to a topic that most authors and pastors avoid: cultural history.

"Some of us were trained that money is dangerous, that prosperity is suspicious, that wealth is reserved for others. Others were told to 'wait on the Lord' while never receiving teaching on planning, discipline, or purpose. Both mindsets kept us poor. Both kept us asking for crumbs while God planned estates."

I urged them to divorce from survival thinking—the thinking that views money as for bills, scraps, and emergencies, and to adopt Kingdom thinking, which perceives that money is for building, empowering, restoring, and establishing households.

I spoke sympathetically now, but more sharply: "God is not increasing you to make you impressive. He is increasing you to make you useful. He is not blessing you so you can show off. He is blessing you so you can build something that remains."

I observed yet another shift as people moved their pens faster, their heads no longer nodding but absorbing. People were realizing that money is not their personal miracle, it is God's ministry flowing through them.

Then I gave the benediction of assignment:

"God's financial blueprint is not about creating wealthy people, it is about creating responsible stewards who free others. God wants you to walk into increase not so you can sit in self-comfort, but so you can reach down, pull someone else up, and change the economic destiny of a family, a community, a people."

The silence that filled the room afterward was not confusion nor wonder; it was conviction. It was agreement. It was understanding. It was calling.

I carefully closed my Bible and noted, "Next week, we will talk about the ninth spiritual law of money—faithfulness—because God does not require perfection to bless you, but He does require consistency."

And as the workshop attendees packed up their belongings, I could tell something had broken through and changed them forever. People walked out not dreaming of wealth, but dreaming of purpose.

THE NINTH
SPIRITUAL LAW OF MONEY

CHAPTER FIFTEEN

The Spiritual Law of Faithfulness

The next week's workshop session at the Empowerment Center filled once again, but this time, something in the air was very different. People walked in early, not late. They took their seats with notebooks open, hearts attentive, ears hungry. They were beginning to understand that these sessions weren't lectures, they were spiritual alignments.

I stepped forward, Bible in hand, and watched the room settle into quiet attention and anticipation.

"Family," I began, "tonight we enter one of the most underestimated but most decisive Spiritual Laws in the Kingdom's financial system—the Spiritual Law of Faithfulness."

I allowed the group's silence to breathe for a moment.

"Faithfulness," I said slowly, "is not tested in the seasons where everything is increasing—it is proven in the seasons where nothing seems to be moving."

I opened the Bible to **Luke 16:10** and read with deliberate emphasis: *Whoever can be trusted with very little can also be trusted with much....*

I lifted my eyes from the page, saying.

"That is Heaven speaking—not Wall Street, not the banks, not financial institutions. God increases based on trustworthiness—not talent, not begging, not desperation."

Heads nodded. Some whispered "Amen."

"I need you to hear me," I continued.

"Faithfulness is the invisible glue. Without it, discipline becomes temporary.

"Generosity becomes sporadic.

"Budgeting becomes intellectual, not transformational.

"Purpose becomes theory—not destiny.

"Faithfulness is the proof that you will not abandon God the moment circumstances shift."

I continued in plain words:

"Faithfulness is showing up for your stewardship when nobody watches you.

"Faithfulness is honoring God's principles when your feelings are in opposition to His instructions.

"Faithfulness is managing what you already have before you ask Heaven to release more.

"In our community, we have been taught how to survive under pressure—but not always how to steward with consistency."

I pointed out that survival suggests, "I just need to make it to next month," while faithfulness evokes, "I will plant for a harvest I cannot yet see."

I continued speaking. "Some of us learned inconsistency because our parents did the best they knew—not because they didn't want better, but because no one taught them to expect better."

The room shifted in discomfort; you could feel people confronting their history.

"But tonight," I declared, "we break that inheritance. We decide that every blessing placed in our hands we will multiply, not squander."

Then I offered a truth that doesn't spark shouting but summons self-examination.

"Heaven accelerates toward people who prove they will not waste increase.

"Some people pray for six figures, but mishandle three.

"Some ask for business expansion, but ignore the discipline required to manage growth.

"Some want wealth, but live as if money is a moment, not a responsibility."

Gently, I asked: "Why would God pour gallons into hands that leak cups?"

No one answered; they just received my question.

I transitioned into testimony because faithfulness must be seen, not just preached.

I told them the story of Sister Jamila, the woman who earned $28,000 a year. She tithed faithfully. Budgeted faithfully. Paid down debt faithfully. Nobody applauded her, and her breakthroughs weren't glamorous. But Heaven watched. Her discipline became a sermon louder than her prayers. God moved, and her income doubled.

"Her promotion," I said, "wasn't given because her résumé was perfect, but because her stewardship was."

Faithfulness, I reminded them, is learned, not felt.

"If you only manage money well when you feel motivated," I said, "you are emotional, not faithful."

I shared that faithfulness is:

Tracking the dollars no one sees.

Giving when you feel like withholding.

Following your blueprint when your emotions want to drift.

Refusing to revert just because no one is cheering.

Then I gave them a warning wrapped in love:

"If God increases you before He strengthens you, the blessing will bankrupt you.

"Jobs, inheritances, promotions, and windfalls without faithfulness become destruction dressed as favor.

"So, Heaven waits.

"Not because God withholds, but because God protects."

I let them sit with that before speaking again.

"Some of you are asking God for more, but God is asking you to show Him that you will treat this increase differently than you treated the last one."

I wasn't trying to shame people, I was inviting them to have faith in God.

I spoke calmly, but with deep conviction:

"Faithfulness is the long road of elevation. Anybody can commit for a week. Heaven is looking for people who commit for years."

Then I sealed my point with:

"When God finds a faithful steward, He pours. And when He pours, no system can block it, no enemy can stop it, and no generation will forget it."

I stepped back, allowing that truth to envelope the people in the room.

And then I spoke to their future:

"Next week," I announced, "we will enter a dimension most believers desperately misunderstand—reciprocity, which is the tenth spiritual law of money. Not charity, not emotional giving, but the kind of generosity Heaven multiplies."

The workshop attendees didn't rush out of the room; they remained seated for a few seconds, absorbing what had been spoken, recognizing that faithfulness isn't something to admire, it is something to become.

THE TENTH
SPIRITUAL LAW OF MONEY

CHAPTER SIXTEEN

The Spiritual Law of Reciprocity

At the next workshop session, the room in the Empowerment Center didn't feel like a class; it felt like a place of processing, a place of separation, a place of refining, and a place of provision. People arrived early, some bowed their heads before taking their seats; others clutched their notebooks as though hunger itself had driven them in. They had learned about stewardship, budgeting, discipline, sowing, and manifestation, but now they were about to collide with the law that determines the direction of increase in the Kingdom.

I stepped forward, opened my Bible, and read slowly from **Luke 6:38** so each word could breathe:

Give, and it shall be given unto you; good measure, pressed down, shaken together, and running over....

The Scripture cast over the room like a mantle. I looked around at people's faces and spoke evenly:

"Family, the world gives you a financial system built on interest rates, algorithms, scores, and approvals, but God gives you something far greater: a spiritual economy. God doesn't transact in volume, He transacts in heart."

I let that truth settle among the people.

"There is a law older than Wall Street, older than banking, older than currency itself: the Spiritual Law of Reciprocity. It governs the flow of provision in His Kingdom. It states plainly: 'Whatever you send out, returns.'"

Then I leaned in toward the group.

"But hear me, it is not a business arrangement. God is not a vending machine. You don't push buttons and expect blessings on demand. You don't give to manipulate Him; you give because you trust Him."

The room quieted, the kind of quiet that promotes conviction.

I continued:

"Reciprocity requires two things: a released hand and a clean motive. If you sow only to get, you've already corrupted the soil. But when you sow because you believe God is your Source…what you release becomes multiplied life."

Next I referred them to the ancient story in **1 Kings 17:8–9**; **17:12–14**, and **17:15–16**, the one that still breathes truth.

"Elijah and the widow," I began, pacing slowly. "A woman with nothing but crumbs in her hands. A prophet with nothing but a word from God in his mouth."

I told the story the way I've seen it in life, the way I've lived it. "She is gathering sticks. She is preparing for death. Her last meal. Her last act as a mother. No hope. No plan. And God sent His prophet to her door."

I paused to let the holy paradox sting. "God commanded a miracle to come through the one who had the least. Why? Because abundance always flows through those willing to trust Him with little."

I described the scene: her worn hands, her rationed flour, her empty oil jar, and Elijah's unthinkable request: *Make me a cake first….*

That sentence still cuts, I pointed out. "That is reciprocity in its purest form where Heaven is asking you to release your last for His first. Not to deprive you, but to reveal whether you trust provision more than the Provider.

"When she acted in faith, her jar never emptied. That widow didn't just survive the famine, she became a testimony of God's math."

Then I faced the group: "Some of you are waiting on God's multiplication, while guarding the seed He told you to release."

Lowering my voice, I said, "You cannot reap from a ground you refuse to sow into. You cannot receive from a hand you refuse to open. God cannot multiply what you hoard in fear."

I walked closer to the group, not to condemn, but to awaken. "The enemy cannot stop God from blessing you, but he can intimidate you into withholding the very seed that activates the blessing."

Then I explained what reciprocity really is:

It is God's answer to scarcity.

It is Heaven's technology for increase.

It is how the Kingdom breaks poverty's inheritance.

But I made sure they understood this law is not only financial.

It works on love. You sow compassion, you receive healing.

It works on time. You serve others, God sends help at your need.

It works on forgiveness. You release what hurt you, and God releases what blesses you.

But tonight, we were dealing with resources, so I noted, "Reciprocity says what you make happen for others, God will make happen for you.

"It isn't emotional giving, it is faith giving.

"It is trusting God enough to give out of need, not just out of comfort."

We then shared stories, quiet miracles from among them.

The mother who tithed in scarcity and found unexpected provision.

The retired veteran who gave groceries and had his pantry filled the next week.

The believer who sowed sacrificially and was blessed in ways no paycheck could engineer.

"Family," I said gently, "the reason we give is not to fund buildings, it is to fund transformation. The storehouse you give into must build dignity, not dependency; empowerment, not entitlement; restoration, not ritual."

Then I spoke to the heart of our people, and to the fear that poverty taught us.

"For centuries, we have been trained to clutch the little because the world convinced us more was not coming. That is survival talking. Reciprocity is faith talking."

I stood still at the front and pointed out, "The widow's jar teaches us this: scarcity dissolves when obedience takes over."

Then I gave them a challenge, not emotional, but spiritual:

"Ask God, 'What seed in my hand is supposed to be released?' And when He shows you, don't negotiate, sow it.

"Because reciprocity works.

"Not sometimes.

"Every time."

I closed with a prophetic charge: "Give from faith, not fear. From joy, not calculation. From obedience, not manipulation."

Then, with a steady voice, I spoke about their next journey:

"Next week, we enter the eleventh spiritual law of money—detachment—where we confront wealth itself, and learn why the Giver must always be greater than the gift."

No one rushed out. They remained seated, quietly, recognizing that reciprocity wasn't something to admire…it was something to obey.

THE ELEVENTH
SPIRITUAL LAW OF MONEY

CHAPTER SEVENTEEN

The Spiritual Law of Detachment

By the time the next workshop session started, there was a noticeable difference in the air inside the Empowerment Center. The same people who once walked in here with shoulders heavy from debt and uncertainty were now carrying notebooks, expectation, and something new—hope. It was as if their hearts were beginning to believe that maybe God's blueprint for financial freedom was not just holy language, but something ordinary people like them could actually live.

I stood before them, Bible open, feeling the weight of everything we had walked through together. We had talked about the discipline of saving, the courage to face debt, the beauty of generosity, the persistence of budgeting, the acceleration of manifestation. We had walked through the laws of sowing, reaping, increase, obedience, purpose, and reciprocity. They had learned how to manage money, grow money, multiply money, and give money. But tonight, we stepped beyond all of that.

Tonight, we stood at the summit because wealth is not fully understood until you learn how to release it.

I slowly read **1 Timothy 6:6–8** so it could sink into the soul: *True godliness with contentment is itself great wealth, for we brought nothing with us when we came into the world, and we will take nothing with us when we leave.*

The room grew still, and I began to speak.

"Family, this is the highest peak. It is not the conclusion of our journey, but the awakening of a clearer view and a greater understanding of our responsibility.

"This is the Spiritual Law of Detachment—the law that frees you from worshipping what God only meant for you to steward. It is the moment when the house, the business, the job title, the applause, even the money itself, loses its power to control your peace."

I watched faces soften, as though something inside them already knew they needed this. I told them that detachment had nothing to do with apathy nor abandonment.

Detachment did not mean lack of care; it meant lack of captivity.

It meant you stopped clinging to the very things God may be calling you to release.

It meant you understood the greatest truth of money: God is the source, everything else is just a resource.

For years I believed freedom was finally having enough money that I never had to worry again, until I met men with full bank accounts and empty souls, and women whose closets were overflowing but their hearts were starving. Freedom is not abundance. I learned that freedom is reaching the point where you can say, "Lord, if You take it all tomorrow, I will still trust You."

That is when wealth graduates into worship. The test is never when you have nothing; the test is when you finally have what you prayed for. When the business succeeds, when income flows, when you can finally breathe financially, that is when God whispers: "If I ask you to give it away, could you?"

Detachment answers yes.

Detachment releases it before God has to pry it from your grip.

Detachment is mastery, not only of money, but of self.

I told them contentment was one of the rarest riches on Earth. It is the sacred place where whether you have much or little, your spirit doesn't flinch. If markets crash, you don't. If applause fades, your identity stands. If things fall apart, your faith doesn't. That, right there, is wealth that cannot be lost.

When you reach this dimension of detachment, life changes. You stop being driven by accumulation and become guided by assignment. Your question shifts from "How much can I have?" to "How much can God do through me?" Accumulation loses its grip and purpose takes over.

That is when your wealth grows legs.

That is when investments become instruments.

That is when what you build outlives your breathing.

Legacy stops being your name engraved on granite and becomes your obedience engraved on eternity. It becomes empowerment centers, scholarships, missions, land, safe homes, opportunities, and structures that keep lifting people long after nobody remembers who started it. Heaven remembers.

I closed my Bible slowly. "Family, you are now nearing mastery." I told them the moment they could walk away from anything without losing peace, everything changes.

Money stops controlling you and starts serving you. You no longer chase blessing because you have become the blessing. You no longer fear tomorrow because you are connected to the One who owns tomorrow.

That is when God can trust you because nothing He gives you owns you anymore.

I smiled at them—not the teacher's smile, but the brother's smile, the witness's smile. "You have climbed high," I told them. "You are close now."

Then I promised that next week we would step into the twelfth and final spiritual law of money—transference—the law of inheritance, the law of legacy, the law that ensures everything you have learned doesn't end with you but continues through your children and their children's children.

The room didn't erupt. It didn't shout. Instead, it grew still—but it was the stillness of reverence. They were not just learning about money anymore. They were learning how to be free.

THE TWELFTH
SPIRITUAL LAW OF MONEY

CHAPTER EIGHTEEN

The Spiritual Law of Transference

By the time the next workshop date arrived, the Empowerment Center did not feel like the same room we started in months ago. The shoulders that once slumped under the weight of overdue notices now carried quiet confidence. Pens clicked before I even reached the podium. These people were no longer hearers. They had become doers. And today, they were ready for the final spiritual law of money.

I walked slowly to the front, Bible pressed to my chest, and opened the book to **Proverbs 13:22**. My voice softened—but was firm as I read: *A good person leaves an inheritance for their children's children.*

The room grew still. You could hear people breathing. The weight of that Scripture landed differently now. We had walked through discipline, faithfulness, budgeting, intentionality, reciprocity, detachment—every law was a rung in a ladder. Now we had climbed to the top.

"Family," I said, "this—right here—is the final spiritual law of money: transference. This is not about how much you earn. It is about how much outlives you."

I watched their eyes widen with thought. Some were thinking about their own parents. Some were thinking about their children. Some were thinking about the absence of inheritance in their bloodline.

I leaned in and gently said, "We have been trained to survive. But the Word tells us to transfer. To pass on. To leave something behind that keeps living after we are gone."

The silence grew thick—holy almost. I told them the truth that many never hear in church:

"You cannot obey God's command to leave an inheritance if you spent your life mismanaging what He gave you. If you wasted your seed, there will be no harvest for your children to pick from. If you broke every spiritual law we walked through, you will leave your children bills instead of blessings."

Then I softened my message, "But for those who have obeyed, who have been faithful, who have grown wealth through wisdom—your work is not finished once you reach overflow. Wealth is not complete until it is secured, protected, directed, and transferred."

I reminded them that Hebrews says it is appointed unto man once to die. That Ecclesiastes declares we enter naked and leave empty-handed. That one day—whether we want to acknowledge it or not—our time will expire.

"The day will come," I said, "when the accounts you fought to balance will outlive you. Your name will be called home. The question Heaven asks is not whether you accumulated—but whether you prepared."

I told them there are only two ways wealth moves after death—by order or by chaos. Families are either blessed by intentional planning, or broken by neglect. And we, as a people, have buried too many mothers and fathers without wills, without instructions, without structure—just tears, confusion, and debt left behind.

The Spiritual Law of Transference is Heaven's command that what God gave you keeps working for His Kingdom long after your pulse stops.

I began to move, pacing and sweeping the room with my eyes. "I cannot tell you how many families I have seen torn apart because someone died without direction. Brothers stopped speaking. Sisters fought. Cousins disappeared. Because nobody taught the deceased this law."

I explained that God provided earthly tools—wills, trusts, titles, beneficiary designation and told them that over 70 percent of African Americans die without a will, leaving the state to divide what God entrusted to them.

"Family," I said quietly but firmly, "we cannot spend our entire life fighting systems that oppressed us only to hand our estate over to the same system when we leave this world. We must secure what God gave us."

Then I recounted the spiritual mystery that always stirs people when they finally hear it—that God Himself practices the law He teaches. God wrote His Will—His covenant Word. God established His Living Trust—Christ Jesus, the mediator of our inheritance. God appointed the Holy Spirit as executor—ensuring what was promised is carried out.

"God didn't just leave us hope," I said, "He left us structure. Heaven didn't risk confusion over who receives the inheritance—why should you?"

That truth broke some people. I saw tears. I saw conviction. I saw resolve.

I leaned forward and almost whispered, "Legacy is not built by what you possess. It is built by what you prepare."

I told them legacy means your grandchildren rise because you rose. Legacy means scholarships built in your name. Legacy means land stays in your bloodline. Legacy means that businesses birthed through you continue to birth others. Legacy means God keeps multiplying the seed you sowed long after your heart stops beating.

I ended quietly, but with a weight that could not be ignored:

"You now know all 'Twelve Spiritual Laws of Money.' You know how to earn, manage, multiply, protect, purify, and release wealth. Now, you must secure it. Because eternity will expose the truth—whether your family was blessed by your life, or burdened by your absence."

The room did not applaud. They bowed their heads instead. A holy hush settled. They were no longer thinking about their accounts—they were thinking about their heirs. They were thinking generationally.

I closed the workshop by saying, "A life well lived is not measured by what you accumulated—but by what Heaven continues to harvest after you are gone. This is your final stewardship test. Leave something behind that makes God smile."

And with that, their financial stewardship journey came full circle—not ending, but beginning again in the next generation.

CHAPTER NINETEEN
Teach What You Have Been Taught

If you have journeyed through these pages, if you have walked through every spiritual law of money, wrestled with old mindsets, confronted habits that kept you bound, opened your heart to truth, and dared to believe that God has a financial blueprint for your life, then you stand at a significant turning point.

You are no longer the person who started reading.

You have been taught.

You have been stretched.

You have been awakened.

That awakening is not just for you—it is a responsibility to others.

God never pours revelation into a heart so it can sit in silence. He pours it so it can overflow. Everything you have learned about discipline, obedience, stewardship, budgeting, sowing, investing, legacy, purpose and detachment must now leave these pages and enter the world through you. The blessing cannot stop at your life. It must pass beyond your life.

You now carry a truth that too many in your family and community do not know. You now hold a revelation that could break cycles, cancel debt, stir faith, rebuild households, and resurrect dreams.

This knowledge cannot die in your notebook. You must become a teacher. A witness. A steward of knowledge. Heaven will one day ask what you did with what you were given. Not just the money you acquired, but the insight that produced it.

Train your children in these laws. Speak life into your family gatherings. Pour wise advice into the young woman who feels defeated by bills. Teach the young man who has never seen wealth handled with dignity. Share with elders who lived their whole life surviving but never thriving. Build circles where conversations about wealth are sacred, not shameful. Stand up in community spaces, living rooms, barbershops, churches and classrooms and declare that God has a plan for His people, and you are walking proof.

Do not wait for perfection to start. Teach from your scars as much as from your victories. Tell people where you failed, where you disobeyed, where you wasted God's blessing, and tell them how God picked you up and rebuilt you through His blueprint. Your story is not a liability; it is a ministry. Your transformation is not private; it is assignment for you to share.

Financial freedom under God is not achieved when you have wealth; it is achieved when you multiply wealthy people. It is not fulfilled when you break the cycle for yourself; it is fulfilled when you break it for someone else. The blueprint is not complete until the student becomes the disciple.

Therefore, go now and teach.

Speak boldly.

Live responsibly.

Model what you preach.

Let your life be the loudest sermon.

Let your household become the first classroom.

Let your obedience be the curriculum.

Let your progress be encouragement to someone still struggling.

Pass on what Heaven passed to you. Rebuild families. Restore dignity. Heal generational wounds. Lift someone who never thought freedom was possible. Because to whom much is given—revelation, wisdom, strategy, grace—much will be required.

God did not direct you to this book so you could get ahead. He acted so you could lead others forward.

Do it with humility.

Do it with courage.

Do it with compassion.

And when God asks who taught His people how to break the spirit of lack, let your name be among the number who answered, "Here I am, Lord. I taught them what You taught me."

Now go.

Live it, teach it, multiply it, and build the legacy Heaven ordained for you to leave.

About The Author

Ananiah Clark is a visionary author, dynamic speaker, and co-founder of PUSH To Be Great, Inc., a national movement dedicated to breaking generational cycles of financial struggle and rebuilding true wealth within Black communities. A proud U.S. Army veteran, Ananiah brings the discipline, resilience, and leadership honed through military service into every environment he enters—empowering individuals to rise above limitations and step boldly into their God-given potential.

His professional experience spans impactful service in the federal government and leadership roles within Fortune 100 companies, where he mastered the ability to dismantle complex systems and transform them into simple, practical, and accessible strategies for everyday people. Educationally, he holds an Associate of Arts, a Bachelor of Arts in Religious Studies, a Bachelor of Arts in Africana Studies, and a Master of Arts in Religion—a powerful combination that enriches his voice in financial education, personal transformation, cultural understanding, and faith-based empowerment.

An anointed preacher, teacher, spiritual advisor, financial coach, entrepreneur, and passionate community advocate, Ananiah bridges the often-overlooked gap between faith and finances. His philosophy is clear: wealth is more than money—wealth is purpose, discipline, identity, legacy, and freedom. Whether through books, workshops, or speaking engagements, he blends soulful storytelling with actionable strategies that help African Americans reclaim their physical, mental, emotional, spiritual, and financial power—without fear, shame, or intimidation.

Known for his bold truth-telling, compassionate leadership, and transformative wisdom, Ananiah challenges his audience to break generational barriers, embrace discipline, and walk with confidence into the life they were created to live. His message is both timely and timeless: you already possess the power to create change, build wealth, and leave a legacy—now is the time to rise and use it.

Widely regarded as an expert in economic empowerment, community development, spiritual growth, and life skills mastery, Ananiah is the author of three influential books:

- *The Money Mentor: A Woman's Guide to Money Mastery*
- *The Money Mentor: A Man's Guide to Money Mastery*
- *Master Your Money: A Roadmap to Financial Freedom*

He resides in Charlotte, North Carolina, with his wife, Berdetta. Together, they share four children—Zyale, Devin, Iyanah, and Keyanla—a daughter-in-love, Mica, and four grandchildren: Zyaire, Jai, Aarionna, and Marlei.

www.ingramcontent.com/pod-product-compliance
Lightning Source LLC
Chambersburg PA
CBHW071119090426
42736CB00012B/1951